583

D1243375

Conrad W. Thomas is himself one of the 31 million private investors for whom this book was written. While still enjoying a career as international mining engineer and consultant, he decided that his deepening interest in the theoretical as well as the practical aspects of investment and asset management made a return to academia desirable. As a Ford Foundation New Careers Fellow, he enrolled at Columbia University's graduate school of business administration. Concentrating on the field of finance, he emerged with a Master of Business Administration degree and (he admits) a more impressive vocabulary.

In 1967, while still at Columbia, he became interested in hedge funds. His conviction that their techniques, properly used, offered every investor a profit potential superior to that of conventional investment methods led to further research, and finally to the writing of this book. Mr. Thomas is currently working on a book devoted entirely to short selling, tentatively titled HOW TO SELL SHORT WITHOUT LOSING YOUR WIFE AND KIDS, FRIENDS AND MISTRESSES.

Hedgemanship*

CONRAD W. THOMAS

1970

DOW JONES-IRWIN, INC.
HOMEWOOD, ILLINOIS

© Conrad W. Thomas

*How to make money in bear markets, bull markets, and chicken markets while confounding professional money managers and attracting a better class of women

39828

© CONRAD W. THOMAS, 1970

All rights reserved. No part of this publication may
be reproduced, stored in a retrieval system, or trans-
mitted, in any form or by any means, electronic,
mechanical, photocopying, recording, or otherwise,
without the prior written permission of the copyright
holder.

First Printing, September, 1970

Library of Congress Catalog Card No. 73-128706
Printed in the United States of America

*To
my wives,
past and future,
without whose absence
this book could never
have been written*

Preface

THE SEARCH for the most appropriate title for this book continued throughout its writing—and indeed the matter is still undetermined as we revise this Preface. At this point, we're more than willing to leave the choice to the editor, who may find some help in the following notes on the book's objectives and a few examples of the titles we have already considered. The titles range from "Hedge Fund Techniques for Every Investor" to the somewhat longer but much more descriptive "How to Make Money in Bear Markets, Bull Markets, and Chicken Markets While Confounding Professional Money Managers and Attracting a Better Class of Women."

The term *chicken market* may need some explanation, for we have just coined it. You already know that a bear market is one that is going down, and a bull market is one that is going up. *What characterizes a chicken market is that no one knows where it is going.* It might be holding fairly still (roosting, one might say), jumping up and down in about the same spot, edging sideways, or simply about to run off unpredictably in any direction.

It is remarkable that Wall Street did not come up with the chicken label at the same time it began to separate the bulls from the bears, for a moment's reflection will confirm that the chicken market is—and always has been—the type of market which prevails most of the time. This is particularly true for the shorter term, and it applies even more specifically to any trading day on which an investment decision must be made— a decision which calls for projecting the current market into the future.

Bear markets and bull markets, especially as to duration, are usually identified *only after they have ended.* (To illustrate: many hedge fund managers were afraid to sell short in the *middle* of the 1969 bear market; they wanted to wait until they were sure the trend would *continue.*) Retrospective market identification, or 20/20 hindsight, is of little value in the buy or sell decision-making process; all that really matters is what will happen in the future. Even the most sustained bull and bear markets will reach an end in the course of a single trading day. Every day brings the same question: Is today that day? Oddly enough, investor opinion on this important matter is about evenly divided. Every day the number of shares bought exactly equals the number of shares sold.

Happily, the investment techniques which have been used (and misused) by hedge funds, as we shall demonstrate in this book, are ideally tailored for chicken markets—and are equally well-suited for making maximum profits in bull markets and bear markets.

As far as we know now, this will be the first book to be published on the subject of hedge funds—those funds that "hedge" their long positions in some stocks by taking short positions in others. Although the private hedge funds have been dubbed "mutual funds for the rich," there is no reason at all why ordinary investors, of whatever degree of affluence, should not employ hedge fund techniques in managing their own resources. There are even certain important advantages in the do-it-yourself operation over an investment in the private or public hedge funds—even those which are well-managed.

Hedge funds, both private and public, have been proliferating in response to strong demand—but to date, unfortunately, the growth rate of the funds has far outstripped the availability of information about them. Lately, because of the dismal performance records of most of them during the 1969 bear market, the hedge funds have lost much of their glamour —but none of their mystery. This mystery apparently extends in some cases to the professional hedge fund managers themselves. As we shall see, their poor performance records can be traced in large part to misuse, ignorance, or abandonment of the basic principles which give the hedge funds their superior profit potential.

The hedge fund does, in fact, offer certain advantages over the ordinary mutual fund as an investment vehicle for pursuing capital gains. In this era of performance-oriented investors, therefore, it seems logical that the private funds, as well as the public open-end investment companies *which successfully use hedge fund techniques,* are destined to grow faster than the ordinary mutual funds.

However, this book is aimed primarily at the individual investors in common stock—who now number nearly 31 million in the United States alone. Even those who may not wish to use all of the techniques employed by hedge fund managers should at least know how to protect themselves, and even profit, when stock prices go down.

Although this book was written with the individual investor primarily in mind, the manager or trustee of *any* fund —pension, trust, foundation, or whatever—might well study the feasibility of applying hedge fund methods to at least some part of the assets in order to improve the rate of capital appreciation. Even if the rules under which a money manager now operates exclude such hedge fund techniques as short selling and debt leverage, he should at least understand the impact of hedge funds on the markets in which he is a competitor. One mutual fund, at least, has changed its charter to allow it to operate as a hedge fund.

Many money managers, notably the upper hierarchy of brokers, have seized upon the private hedge fund as a means of multiplying their own capital. It was with this group in mind that it occurred to us to call the book "Why Brokers Invest Their Own Money in Hedge Funds." The title is attention-getting, and we explore the subject, but it takes up only a small part of the book.

Another title considered, "Refresher Course for Hedge Fund Managers Who Somehow Forgot," might have alienated some of the professionals, which we would not care to do, for the possibility does exist that certain parts of this book could serve some useful purpose for those hedge fund managers who appear to have strayed—as we have already noted—from the basic principles of successful hedge fund operation, and who might wish to review those principles. In the same spirit of humility we also offer some devices of our own invention which we believe might be useful even to the pros, including "The Gunslingers of Wall Street," to mention another title they probably wouldn't care for.

All investors—present and potential—in the private and public hedge funds run by the pros might well benefit from a more thorough understanding of how these funds operate. Performance alone—even when the performance is commendable—does not tell the whole story; also important are the risks involved and the cost of management—usually 20 percent of net gain in assets for the private partnerships, and up to 4 percent of the total assets managed in the case of some public hedge funds. These figures alone might well inspire the individual investor to manage his own hedge fund.

Hedge funds have already come under the obviously concerned scrutiny of the Securities & Exchange Commission as well as the regulatory bodies of the New York and American Stock Exchanges. Given the strong probability of a continuing rapid growth of the funds, and their acknowledged impact on the stock market, it seems likely that the future will bring at least some increase in regulation—and perhaps even legislation aimed specifically at hedge funds. In any case, a much wider understanding of just what hedge funds are—and are not—can only benefit their healthy development.

Returning to our quest for an appropriate title, we must admit that "Hedge Fund Techniques for Every Investor" is not likely to quicken the pulse of many of the 31 million private investors for whom this book was written. The title is in fact incomplete, for it carries little hint of the book's range and treatment, which is quite unlike anything the author ever came across in business school—or anywhere else, come to think of it.

Another objection to the title "Hedge Fund Techniques for Every Investor" is that so few people now understand what a hedge fund is, or what it should be—and that statement applies not only to the general investing public, but to some investors in, and managers of, hedge funds. Even knowing what the term *hedging* means is no help, for the hedge funds do not—or should not—use true hedging, as it is commonly understood. We need a new term—*hedgery* or *hedgemanship*, perhaps.

What title, then, would attract the wider readership at which the book is aimed? We considered, fleetingly, "Sex and the Single Investor." With an appropriately lustful nude on the dust jacket, and displayed among the current best-selling porno output, book sales would no doubt be stimulated. Some buyers, however, might get the impression they had been misled. Only a limited number, we feel, would get much of a charge out of what is probably the book's most erotic word, "shorts"—even when the shorts come down, as they do herein under favorable circumstances. We do mention "masochism" at one point and "consenting adults" at another, but only in relation to unsuccessful short sellers and high management fees, respectively.

This book *is* concerned with making money, and the word "money," of course, is considered pretty sexy, especially by women. Certainly no one can doubt that the possession of it in appreciable quantities can increase a man's attractiveness in the eyes of a woman. Consider the case of the gorgeous widow and that shipping fellow—somewhat less gorgeous, in our opinion—who . . . well, you know the story.

Another title we considered, "The Gentleman's Guide to Avarice-Satisfaction," is fairly relevant, but too narrow.

We liked "How to Run Your Own Hedge Fund and Other Stories," but decided to save it for our memoirs—or the musical version of the book.

To get the attention of the graduate schools of business administration, we thought of something along the lines of

"An Analysis of Partial Optimization of Certain Investment Fund Portfolios." Although the author himself first became interested in hedge funds in the course of obtaining an MBA degree from Columbia, it was not during a course on the subject of hedge funds. No such course existed. Perhaps the subject will be given some attention in the future. The growth predicted for hedge funds will certainly create a need for more career managers. Naturally, competence in fund management can come only with actual experience in the marketplace, but the schools could at least review the fundamentals for those students interested in such a career.

We must note, however, that a course in hedge fund management would be more practical than most of those offered today in graduate schools of business, which are becoming more and more theory-oriented. We shall never forget one course we attended which was presided over by a bright young Indian scholar, something of a mystic, we finally concluded. The course was called, forthrightly enough, "Financial Management," but as it was revealed to us it seemed to have more in common with Zen than with any practices presently known to the financial community.

We can't deny that we left business school with a more impressive vocabulary, but in order to serve the potential readership mentioned, we have endeavored to keep our presentation as simple and informal as possible, consistent with the goal of adequately informing. Consequently, we have— not without some regret—eschewed sly references to, and ostentatious use of, multiple regression analysis, differential equations, mathematical models for portfolio analysis, simulation, Markowitz's efficient combinations, and other graduate school impedimenta which might excite the reader's awe but dull his perception. We trust this sacrifice has not been made in vain.

Los Angeles, California   CONRAD W. THOMAS
August, 1970

A note about notes and sources

THERE are no footnotes in this book. The "superior" numbers (numbers placed above the line) which appear throughout the text are used to indicate the author's sources of quotations and other information from published sources. The numbers do not appear in numerical order, and some are repeated. Their appearance need not halt the rush of the reader's eye—unless, of course, he wishes to check a source or read more on the subject, in which case he can refer to the list at the end of the text.

The numbers all refer to articles published in magazines and newspapers—practically everything (except prospectuses) that has been printed to date about hedge funds. The articles are arranged chronologically, the oldest first. Some idea of the brief history of hedge funds can be obtained simply by reading down the list of headlines.

Only the first three articles on the list, all published in 1966, had appeared before the author became interested in hedge funds and wrote term papers on the subject for investment and banking courses in graduate school. A possible indication of the paucity of, and demand for, information on hedge funds may be gained from the fact that one of the papers disappeared from the office of the professor for whom it was written. The author would like to believe that the paper's title, "A Critical Examination of Hedge Funds," proved irresistible to some younger fellow-student (they were *all* younger), who is now, two years later, one of the hottest young hedge fund managers on Wall Street.

If the reader wishes to review any of the source materials in their entirety, he can probably find the bound magazines in most large public or university libraries, or in the libraries of graduate schools of business. Back issues of *The Wall Street Journal* are usually available on microfilm.

Contents

section **ONE**
A little background music

section **FIVE**
Do-it-yourself and the alternatives

section ONE

A little background music

What is a hedge fund?

INTRODUCTION TO HEDGE FUNDS

THERE IS no general agreement as yet on exactly what a hedge fund is. The term is applied by some only to *private* investment partnerships, while *public* hedge funds are referred to rather lengthily as "open-end investment companies (commonly known as mutual funds) that use hedging techniques."

Two public funds, Hedge Fund of America and Tudor Hedge Fund, are clearly labeled. Other mutual funds which use hedge fund methods may not have the words *Hedge Fund* in their titles, but do not deny that they are in fact hedge funds. Still others, using the same basic techniques, seem to prefer not being classed as hedge funds.

Except for certain important details regarding regulation, taxation, and restrictions on operations—to be discussed later —the private and public hedge funds are essentially alike. For the purpose of this book, any fund, whether public or private, that takes long positions in some stocks and short positions in others will be called a hedge fund.

A DEFINITION

A more formal definition is as follows: A hedge fund is a private or public pool of investment capital which seeks to minimize risk by "hedging" its long positions in some stocks by taking short positions in other stocks, and which usually

3

pursues its goal of maximum capital appreciation by employing leverage to maximize performance.

NOT A TRUE HEDGE

Note that the long positions in some stocks are "hedged" by short positions in other, unrelated stocks. The hedge fund, therefore, is not a true hedge.

A *true* hedge is one involving related securities of the same company; for example, common stock, convertible preferred stock, convertible bonds, when-issued stock, or put and call options. A change in the price of the common would be reflected by a related price move in the other securities of the company. An example of a true hedge would be a long position in the convertible bond and a short position in exactly the number of shares into which the bond is convertible.

The true hedge can be useful in arbitrage and for other purposes, but should not normally be used by a hedge fund, because its use would detract from leverage.

HEDGE FUND HEDGING

Although the type of hedging employed by the hedge fund is intended to reduce risk, *it cannot eliminate risk*. The longs can go down; the shorts can go up. The need for proper selection and timing is not eliminated by the hedge formula.

Of course, the fund manager tries to select longs that will go up and shorts that will go down, and if his judgment on his selections and the overall market is good, fund appreciation will result.

However, this ideal situation need not be realized for the fund to make money. The manager selects longs that he believes will rise more than the average in a generally rising market, and fall less than the average in a generally falling market. He selects shorts that will drop faster than the average in a falling market, and rise less than the average in a rising market. Even if he misjudges the general trend of the market, he is partially sheltered by being both long and short.

The manager of a conventional fund—a mutual fund, for example—adjusts the relative proportions of stocks (all longs) and cash according to his assessment of market risk. In contrast, the hedge fund manager abhors idle cash, stays fully invested at all times, and attempts to minimize risk by adjusting the relative proportions of longs and shorts in his portfolio in accord with his assessment of market risk.

THE HEDGE FUNDER'S "RISK"

Herein "risk" (in quotation marks) denotes the hedge funder's definition, which is simply the difference between the long and the short positions as a percentage of the paid-in, or unleveraged, capital—it is not the same as risk in the normal sense. For example, if the fund has $100,000 paid-in capital and adds $50,000 more by borrowing, the manager might decide to go long $110,000 on stocks he thinks will go up and go short $40,000 on stocks he thinks are overvalued. The unsheltered or unhedged investment is therefore $110,000 minus $40,000, or $70,000; and the "risk" is $70,000 divided by $100,000, or 70 percent.

If the longs and shorts were equally divided (each one $75,000 in this case), the "risk," as defined, would be zero. Finally, if the shorts exceeded the longs by $70,000, the "risk" would be *minus* 70 percent.

THE PRAGMATIC APPROACH

The relative proportions of longs and shorts, as we have noted, depend on the manager's assessment of the market and its predominant direction. In strong bull markets, the longs predominate; in precipitous bear markets, the shorts. In sideways or uncertain (chicken) markets the longs and shorts may be about equal.

Note that the hedge fund manager need not make elaborate forecasts based on such factors as economic conditions, the trend of interest rates, inflation, taxes, war, peace, sunspots, or how he's getting along with his wife. He can simply adjust the proportion of his longs and his shorts to keep in tune with market conditions as they are revealed to him.

THE HEDGE FUNDER'S "VELOCITY"

Some hedge fund managers use what they call a "velocity" factor—a measure of price volatility—to obtain a more sensitive measure of "risk." Each stock in the portfolio is assigned a velocity rating according to its chart activity compared to some standard over a certain period of time; Standard & Poor's 500-stock average is commonly used as the base.

General Electric, for example, might rate a velocity of 1.5, while something like Pizzatronics would rate a 7. The dollar sum invested in each stock, long or short, is multiplied by the velocity, then the adjusted long and short positions are totaled, and the resultant "risk" is determined. Examples of velocity factors and the method of calculating the adjusted "risk" will be given later.

The remarkable performance
of the man who started it all

UNTIL 1966 the general investing public, as well as most of the professionals, had no knowledge at all of the marvelous investment device called the hedge fund. In April of that year, however, both *Fortune*[1] and *Business Week*[2] published articles on the private investment partnerships originated by Alfred Winslow Jones, who, after obtaining a PhD degree in sociology—not business—at Columbia University, had served as director of its Institute of Applied Social Analysis, and had also done some book and magazine writing.

The *Fortune* article was aptly titled "The Jones Nobody Keeps Up With." *Nobody* meant not even Fidelity Trend Fund and Dreyfus Fund, which had posted the best records among mutual funds during the previous 5- and 10-year periods, respectively. In the 5-year period Jones had outgained Fidelity Trend, then managed by Gerald Tsai, by 325 percent to 225 percent in capital appreciation (assuming reinvestment of capital gains and dividends). In the 10-year period Jones did nearly twice as well as Dreyfus—670 percent to 358 percent.

Jones' record appears even more impressive in light of the fact that his figures represent gains to investors (limited partners) in his funds *after* he had withdrawn 20 percent off

7

the top of net gain as a reward for his efforts and those of his general, or management, partners.

Obviously, Jones had a good thing going. Others privy to the record thought so too. Not only was there a press of the knowing rich to get richer, but some of Jones' associates thought that *he* was doing quite well also; they dropped out to start hedge funds of their own. Wall Street scuttlebutt is that some of these half dozen or so Jones alumni have done even better than the "old master," as he has been dubbed by *Dun's Review*.[4] The same magazine reports that the Old Master (surely the title deserves capitalization) "is reputed to take home something in the millions each year."

The indefinite nature of the last statistic is somehow typical of the state of information about hedge funds. But if the streets are paved with gold, who is base enough to quibble about the exact number of streets? They were soon to become crowded.

The explosive growth
of the hedge funds

ONLY A HANDFUL of private hedge funds existed at the time the *Fortune* and *Business Week* articles appeared in April 1966, and there were no public hedge funds at all. In spite of the demand for his services, Jones accepted only a few new limited partners each year, and even these few generally had close connections with the existing partners. The *Fortune* piece reported that there were about 60 investors in Jones' two funds, their average share being about $460,000.

Two of Jones' former associates were already running their own hedge funds under the names of City Associates and Fairfield Partners. Even brokers who had done business with Jones decided to get into the act; one group started Fleschner Becker Associates. Besides those named, *Fortune* noted a number of other hedge funds operating on a small scale.

Business Week added to the list: three hedge funds run by John Hartwell, a New York investment advisor, other funds in Philadelphia and Boston, "several family operations run on hedge fund principles," and "at least two" private hedge funds run by "well-known brokerage houses."

"Several partnerships have opened for business in the past two weeks," the magazine reported. The boom in hedge funds was under way.

And now, for the first time, the general public was to have

9

access to the joys of hedge fund participation. The Hubshman Fund, whose broker principals had also done business with Jones, had filed with the Securities & Exchange Commission (SEC) a registration statement as an open-end investment company, or mutual fund. Departing from the usual mutual fund pattern up to that time, the new fund stated its intention of employing hedge fund techniques.

The Hubshman Fund, after protracted discussions with the SEC over the content and wording of its prospectus, finally got started in November 1966. It was quickly followed the next year by the Hartwell & Campbell Fund, the Blair Fund, and the Heritage Fund, which converted from an older, conventional mutual fund.

Hedge Fund of America, described by the *New York Times*[5] as "the first nationwide fund to capitalize on the hedging concept in a big way," appeared in February 1968. The fund was underwritten by Walston & Co., an old-line brokerage house, and soon attracted some $60 million or so in capital. It was followed in March by Competitive Associates, based in San Francisco.

The first part of 1969 saw the advent of Berger-Kent Special Fund, Tudor Hedge Fund, and Dreyfus Leverage Fund, among others, and still more were warming up for public takeoff.

Meanwhile, the private hedge funds were proliferating at a fantastic rate. The Jones boys continued to disperse, setting up their own funds in response to lively demand. *Dun's Review*,[4] in its January 1968 article, "Heyday of the Hedge Funds," noted that the hedge fund "formula, such as it is, has proved readily transferable."

The *Economist*[10] in May 1968 commented on the hedge funds' spectacular growth: "double . . . a year ago, and five times . . . two years ago." The funds were even making news abroad.

In mid-1968 *Barron's*[11] had asked Barton Biggs, of Fairfield Partners, headquartered in moneybagged Greenwich, Connecticut, "Why the sudden interest [in hedge funds]?" Biggs: "I think it's the result of the performance cult. A lot of wealthy people suddenly discovered that their money was being managed very poorly by banks and old-line advisors."

Earlier in the year, in April and May, the *Wall Street Journal*[6, 8] had run stories about increasing concern by the SEC and the New York and American Stock Exchanges over the greatly expanded involvement of exchange members in "private investment partnerships," mainly hedge funds. In the May 20 article, the number of hedge funds with over $1 million in assets was estimated at 100, with a total of $1 billion in assets. On the following day the *Journal*[9] reported that the figures for both number of funds and total assets were up fivefold over the previous year (indicating an even faster growth rate than that estimated by the *Economist*). The article stated that the New York Stock Exchange "estimates that there are some 15 such [broker-run] private funds in operation. Almost all have been formed in recent months."

Further comments will be made on exchange member involvement in hedge fund activities in the following pages. Let us close here with another quote from the *Wall Street Journal*[21] regarding the latest published figures (as of August 1969) on the ballooning hedge funds: "Wall Street estimates place their numbers now at more than 300 and their total assets at between $1 billion and $2 billion."

Who's playing:
stock exchange member firms

HAVE THEY FOUND A BETTER WAY FOR THEMSELVES?

In the previous discussion we mentioned the concern aroused by the heavy involvement of certain New York and American Stock Exchange people in *private* investment partnerships, mainly hedge funds, whose aim is maximum capital appreciation. What is the nature and extent of that involvement?

The *Wall Street Journal*[20] on April 28, 1969 cited a study by the American Stock Exchange (ASE)—which has a 90 percent overlap with the New York Stock Exchange (NYSE) membership—that reported results of a poll of its 580 member firms, and "showed that 158 officers and 80 firms currently are participating in 125 investment partnerships. Total assets in individual funds ranged from $100,000 to $50 million."

The *Journal* piece added, "The exchange didn't give the total assets of all 125 funds, but it's understood that they aggregate about $1 billion." One billion dollars! If that is true, it must follow, as the night the day, that exchange members dominate the bulk of all hedge funds, which latest estimates place somewhere between $1 billion and $2 billion.

The individual private investor, along with others whose business sustains the brokerage houses, may well ask: Have they found a better way of investing their own money than the one they're selling to me?

As the *Economist* phrased it, "American stockbrokers, like others, do the best they can for their customers, but isn't it likely that when investing for themselves the brokers should try to do even better?"

Some of these private funds are producing results that the ordinary brokerage house customer might well envy. The *Wall Street Journal*[8] has reported that "Graham Loving Jr., a partner in Graham Loving & Co., a Big Board member firm, is a general partner of Gralov Associates, a $5 million hedge fund that has shown a 200% capital appreciation since it was formed two years ago." We can't help wondering how many of the firm's customers did as well.

"Among the 19 limited partners in this fund," the *Journal* continues, "is FNS Trading Partnership . . . a unit of First Nebraska Securities Inc., another Big Board firm based in Omaha, Neb." Although First Nebraska has no voice in the fund's management, it apparently has responded to opportunity's knock—a knock that may be less audible to some of its own public customers.

The *Journal*[9] also names some other Big Board member firm partners who operate private hedge funds and other investment partnerships, including A. J. Butler & Co., Donaldson, Lufkin & Jenrett Inc., Oppenheimer & Co., and Burnham & Co., which sponsors a fund for 42 "selected employees" who invest in "special deals" . . . that their "general customers wouldn't go into," as the general partner explained.

The foregoing paragraphs should be enough to convince us that many Wall Street member firm managers and other insiders have been quick to recognize the value of, and to capitalize on, the hedge fund concept, even though the idea did not originate with them. It also appears that a large share of the total capital invested in such private hedge funds comes from this group.

CONFLICT OF INTEREST?

As to whether or not this situation could give rise to conflict of interest and other problems, much of the story is told in the headlines of the *Wall Street Journal:*

Big Board Warns Hedge Fund
Trading Rise Imperils Finances
Of Some Member Firms
(April 3, 1968)

Hedge Funds: Investing
Partnerships Grow, Draw
Scrutiny By Exchanges and SEC
(May 20, 1968)

("The possibility might arise," says the article, "if a broker-age house recommended to its public customers the purchase of a stock that the hedge fund had already invested in. How-ever well-intentioned the recommendation, such purchases would tend to push up the price of the stock, to the hedge fund's benefit.")

American Exchange Starts
Member Poll On Hedge Fund Role
(May 21, 1968)

Securities Regulators
Express Their Concern
About Hedge Funds
(March 10, 1969)

American Board Finds Its Rules
Adequate To Cover Members'
Hedge Fund Activities
(April 28, 1969)

Close Regulation Of Hedge Funds
Is Backed By SEC Staff:
Study Is Now Under Way
(October 22, 1969)

The *Economist,* which apparently follows the *Wall Street Journal* also, summed up the conflict of interest problem in these words:

The funds can, in theory, use their highly geared buying power to move up the price of a stock only to unload their holdings as unsuspecting investors jump on the bandwagon. It would be even worse if the lambs that are thus shorn were customers of a brokerage house that sheltered the hedge fund responsible. And some partners in hedge funds are executives and directors of large corporations and in that capacity have access to information about company affairs not known to most investors that can be useful to the funds in making their investments.

Of course, we know the British reputation for understatement. A less-restrained observer might opine that he did not see how, under the circumstances, conflict of interest could possibly be avoided by any means short of multiple lobotomy.

Not so, say the brokers who run hedge funds. They exercise "constant self-discipline" to avoid conflict of interest situations. "We make sure that when our public customers and the funds are interested in the same situation, the fund comes last," the *Wall Street Journal*[8] quotes Abbey J. Butler, a partner in NYSE member A. J. Butler & Co., which sponsors Butler Fund for nine individuals who anted up $1,150,000 to start their pot boiling.

"We lean the other way to favor our public customers," says Mr. Butler, citing an example in which his firm took a position in Occidental Petroleum for his public customers before buying it later for the fund at a higher price. Moreover, "before Butler Fund sells any stock short," he told the *Journal,* "we advise our other customers that the fund no longer favors that stock."

AN OPPORTUNITY FOR THE ORDINARY CLIENT?

Well, at the very least, the above does suggest how the ordinary customers of such trustworthy, loyal, helpful, friendly, courteous, kind, etc. brokerage houses can manage their own assets by using hedge fund techniques along with the buy, sell and timing information supplied by their brokers. Not only will the customer be relieved of that most difficult task of hedge fund management—stock selection and timing—but he is virtually certain to outperform the private fund run by his own broker.

Right?

Who else is playing:
the rich, the talented,
the sophisticated,
and that fellow in Geneva(?)

BESIDES THOSE fortunate enough to have good connections inside certain exchange member firms, as we have seen earlier in this section, there are many others who have invested in the private hedge funds. Who are they?

Well, hedge funds are not called "mutual funds for the rich" without reason. With individual entrance fees of $100,000 to $500,000 and more, the investor must obviously be fairly well off even to get in the game. The *Fortune* article lists several of Jones' well-heeled clients: the president of Loew's Theatres, the ex-president of Kellwood Co., several Richardsons of Richardson-Merrell, a Mexico City businessman (with $2,-260,000 in one Jones fund), a physician turned sculptor (about $2 million), and a bridge expert with wool money. Captains of industry, creators, thinkers, individualists all—yet all quite willing to risk their capital and pay 20 percent of the profit made on their money in return for the right kind of hedge fund management. In addition, according to *Fortune*, Jones has *made* millionaires of several of his investors who did not enjoy that status from the onset.

Business Week says, "Generally hedge funds have attracted as partners some sophisticated names in U.S. business —corporation presidents, board chairmen and bankers." Yes, bankers. They manage a lot of other people's money, too, don't they? (And note that word *sophisticated*. We shall have more to say on the role of sophistication in hedge fund investment in Section Five.)

The subtitle of the *Business Week* article, in fact, nicely sums up those who are investing, and why: "Smart Wall Street investors are cutting their risk by going into hedge funds—a way to go both long and short, and get top profits while protecting their capital."

Dun's Review[4] adds the tax incentive: As the boom moves along (the article was written in January 1968), "the ranks of U.S. executives boast more and more high-bracket incomes, while ever-climbing taxes intensify the search for a shelter." (The effect of taxes will be discussed later. The shelter is questionable.)

Dun's Review continues: "Today's high-salaried executives (and their recently retired confreres) are among the minority who have the sophistication [there's that word again] that hedge fund investing requires."

The magazine also adds some prominent figures to the list of those interested financially in hedge funds: the chairman of Eversharp (and one-time head of the Strategic Air Command), a former managing director of McKinsey & Co., one of the best-known management consulting firms, a prominent New York lawyer and international figure, a publisher, a Nobel Prize winner and former Atomic Energy Commissioner, and an economic advisor to U.S. presidents. The positions and achievements of these people, rather than their actual names, have been given the emphasis here in order to highlight the caliber of some of those who have a stake in hedge funds.

We have dwelt upon this matter of "Who's Playing" the hedge fund game both as a possible inspiration for the potential entrant and as an introduction to the company he'll be keeping.

But if the hedge game is so hot, some might still protest, why isn't international financial wheeler-dealer Bernie Cornfeld sitting in? The controversial head of Investors Overseas Services (IOS) and Fund of Funds may indeed have placed a small bet. *Forbes*[18] has reported that Maryland-based Computer Directions Advisors, an investment advisory firm, received $200,000 a year from Cornfeld's IOS in Geneva. *Forbes* does not say that the $25 million IOS capital involved (out of its total $1.6 billion) is managed as a hedge fund. The advisor "is not free to reveal his performance for IOS"—but it reports that the advisory service does manage a private hedge fund which "chalked up better than a 40% gain," the sort of performance that just might interest Bernie Cornfeld, at least until all hell breaks loose.

The information gap

FROM their inception, an air of mystery—almost of conspiracy —has surrounded the private hedge funds. The father of the hedge funds, Alfred Winslow Jones, was performing spectacular feats of enrichment for himself and his partners for 17 years before the *Fortune* and *Business Week* articles were published in 1966.

In spite of the fact that Jones' performance in the stock market made him "one of the wonders of Wall Street," few businessmen had even heard of him, said *Fortune,* which characterized him as "quiet spoken, seldom-photographed," but did publish his comments, his performance record, and a photograph. *Dun's Review* refers to Jones' "sphinx-like policy," but in 1968 it found one of his general partners somewhat more communicative about what it called "these little known stock market operators."

As recently as 1968, the *Wall Street Journal* was calling hedge funds "an investment apparatus about which relatively little is known"[6] and "a type of investing partnership the general public as yet knows little about."[8] And as late as March 1969 the *Los Angeles Times*[15] wrote of the "shroud of mystery" surrounding hedge funds.

To be fair to the private funds, it's not their job to keep the public informed. They are, after all, private partnerships, with no legal responsibility to publicize either their methods or their results. To do so, in fact, might be interpreted as solicitation of funds, possibly bringing into question the privacy of the partnership agreements and drawing the attention of the Securities and Exchange Commission, which has been conducting investigations anyway. Neither the regulatory bodies nor the courts have clearly defined the dividing line between private and public investment vehicles, although 100 partners is generally considered the maximum for a private partnership. The private funds try to limit the membership to 20 or 30.

Public hedge funds, like ordinary mutual funds, are registered with and regulated by the SEC, to which they must submit regular reports. Their stockholders, and therefore the general public, also receive periodic reports, including income statements, balance sheets and investment portfolios. The prospectus of the Hubshman Fund, the first of the public hedge funds, was as we have noted finally approved, or allowed to pass, by the SEC in late 1966. Since that time the prospectuses of several other public hedge funds have appeared, and they do make interesting reading.

Can we conclude, then, that the shroud of mystery has lifted? Not much, as we have seen from the comments in the press. In fact, the brume may be even more dense than the newspapers suggest.

Two years ago the author, while attending Columbia's graduate school of business, wrote a paper grandly titled *Hedge Funds, Mutual Funds and Super Funds*, which concluded that a lack of understanding of hedge fund fundamentals is not only widespread among the general investing public, but might even extend to some of the "sophisticated" investors who trust their money to the funds.

With the recent publication of dismal performance records, together with the explanations and comments of some of the managers of the private and public hedge funds involved, there is reason to believe that lack of knowledge may extend even to some of those in the inner circle. (This subject will be developed in Section Five, under the heading The Bear Market Nightmare—Or What Went Wrong?)

What is encouraging, however, is the increasing willingness of hedge fund managers to talk about their operations for the enlightenment of the investing public. Some of them, it is true, seem sometimes to be talking out of both sides of the mouth, but this may be an occupational hazard among those whose professional duties require playing both sides of the street.

Nevertheless, with their help, we can now begin to lift that "shroud of mystery," and attempt to bridge the gap between the booming growth of hedge funds and the lagging pace of information about them.

section TWO

The
performance game

Factors that determine performance

ANYONE who has ever bought and sold stock through a broker and who has made out his own income tax return can sit down and make out a list of factors that determined the profit or loss on his transactions. The list might look like this:

1. Price at which stock was bought
2. Selling price
3. Brokerage commissions and transfer taxes
4. Length of time stock was held, which determines the next item
5. Income tax treatment of capital gain or loss (long- or short-term)
6. Cash dividends received
7. Miscellaneous costs (financial services, publications, etc.)

The above are the only factors that can possibly affect the profit and loss—the performance—of the ordinary investor who does not sell short or borrow money to buy stocks. There is no column on the tax form, for example, headed "Loss claimed due to whipsawing." Except for commissions (over which he has little control), miscellaneous expenses (complete control), and tax *laws* (beyond control), the factors listed can be summed up in the phrase: *stock selection and timing,* which can even affect importantly the amounts of tax and commissions.

While selection and timing are very important in the operation of any funds, hedge funds have added some other factors

—we have already mentioned leverage, hedging and short selling—that may be of comparable importance. The effect of these on the performance of various types of funds under assumed market conditions will be examined in the following pages. The general approach will consist of holding constant some factors while determining the effect of variations in others—all of which will become clear when we get to the first table in the following discussion.

(Managers of hedge funds have cited still other factors that are important in their operations, namely, ready access to sources of information, maneuverability and turnover. These are related to selection and timing, and will be discussed at the end of Section Three.)

Performance of
three hedge funds,
a mutual fund,
and the ordinary investor

INTRODUCTION

In the previous section we examined the performance record of the Old Master of the hedge funds, showing how he outdistanced even the best of the mutual funds. We also outlined the explosive growth of the hedge funds, based upon the demand by investors for such investment management, and indicated the caliber of the people who have a financial stake in the funds.

Now we begin the examination of the fundamental reasons for the superior performance potential of the hedge funds. The word *potential* is important. Some alleged hedge funds, as we shall see in Section Five, have actually managed to turn in *inferior* performances, failing even to match the Dow Jones Industrial Average in a *bear* market, where the odds are in their favor. The reasons will be investigated in the section mentioned, after we have reviewed the fundamentals of successful hedge fund management.

What are those fundamentals?

A good start on the answer can be obtained through the

study of a simple table. This table is so simple, in fact, that it verges on the simple-minded; so if, after we've gone over it, you can say that you knew it all the time, you can then be sure that you have given it the attention it deserves.

In the opinion of the author, the table has up to now been used more to sell than to enlighten. He first had a glimpse of such a table during attendance at business school, where he heard a talk on hedge funds given by a savvy young visiting lecturer from Wall Street, who was then setting up a hedge fund with himself as manager. It was a most convincing spiel, and the table—chalked on the classroom blackboard almost furtively—was the clincher. It was soon erased.

The author's Table 1 is not an exact copy of the one mentioned, but it doesn't really matter. In fact, after he is familiar with Table 1, the reader is encouraged to makes tables of his own, changing the variables as he may wish. All the tables will show the same thing; all will show the superiority of the leveraged hedge funds over the mutual fund and the ordinary investor.

THE FUNDS DESCRIBED

Table 1 shows the quantitative performance of five different types of investment instruments (cash fund, mutual fund, and three variously leveraged hedge funds) under five different hypothetical market movements. Each fund begins each market movement with $100 paid-in capital. (If the reader prefers to think in larger sums, he can add an appropriate number of zeros to the figures given.)

First, a description of the funds themselves:

Fund A, which we call the *Cash Fund,* represents the ordinary investor with all of the funds he has available for the stock market invested long in various stocks; he does no buying on margin. Because the total investment is on the long side, the "risk" for this fund is 100 percent. In other words, 100 percent of his investment would be threatened by a market drop. All other funds in Table 1 have a 70 percent "risk."

TABLE 1

Performances of five fund types under various market conditions
($100 paid-in capital)

	Cash Fund 100% Invested (A)	Mutual Fund 70% Invested (B)	Hedge Funds		
			All Cash (C)	50% Lever- age (D)	100% Lever- age (E)
Invested long	100	70	85	110	135
Invested short (or cash) ..	0	(30)	15	40	65
Risk %	100	70	70	70	70
1. Longs up 30%	+30	+21	+25.5	+33	+40.5
Shorts up 30%			− 4.5	−12	−19.5
Net change	+30	+21	+21	+21	+21
2. Longs down 30%	−30	−21	−25.5	−33	−40.5
Shorts down 30%			+ 4.5	+12	+19.5
Net change	−30	−21	−21	−21	−21
3. Longs up 40%	+40	+28	+34	+44	+54.
Shorts up 10%			− 1.5	− 4	− 6.5
Net change	+40	+28	+32.5	+40	+47.5
4. Longs down 10%	−10	− 7	− 8.5	−11	−13.5
Shorts down 40%			+ 6	+16	+26
Net change	−10	− 7	− 2.5	+ 5	+12.5
5. Longs up 30%	+30	+21	+25.5	+33	+40.5
Shorts down 30%			+ 4.5	+12	+19.5
Net change	+30	+21	+30	+45	+60
Average return %	12	8.4	12	18	24
Cumulative return %..	60	42	60	90	120

Fund B represents the ordinary *Mutual Fund,* which cannot use short selling or debt leverage. It tries to protect itself during downside market movements by increasing its cash position (or by buying interest-bearing "near-cash" securities such as short-term Treasury issues). In order to achieve a "risk" position comparable to the 70 percent of the three hedge funds shown in the table, the Mutual Fund would have 30 percent of its total funds in cash, and 70 percent invested long. Thirty percent is a much higher cash position than most mutual funds carry even when the outlook is very bearish.

Just like the ordinary individual investor, the mutual fund managers are often locked into stocks showing big paper losses caused by sudden dips or prolonged bear markets. Moreover, the managers of the larger mutual funds may hold positions in some stocks of a size that makes rapid liquidation difficult or impossible.

The three remaining funds shown in the table are hedge funds, all with the same "risk" of 70 percent, but different amounts of debt leverage. These differences will serve to highlight the effect of leverage, a very important factor in hedge fund performance.

The first of this group, Fund C, is a hedge fund using no debt leverage at all. It takes a short position of 15 percent in order to hedge its 85 percent long position, resulting in 70 percent "risk" $(85 - 15 = 70)$. We call it the *Cash Hedge Fund.*

Fund D, called the *50% Hedge Fund,* increases its original capital of $100 by 50 percent through various methods of leveraging: buying on margin, other borrowing, etc. (Methods of leveraging will be developed in detail later.) The 50% Hedge Fund is long 110 percent (of the unleveraged capital) and short 40 percent, resulting in the desired 70 percent "risk" $(110 - 40 = 70)$.

Finally, Fund E, the *100% Hedge Fund,* doubles its paid-in capital by leveraging, and invests 135 percent long and 65 percent short, with the risk remaining at 70 percent $(135 - 65 = 70)$.

FUND PERFORMANCE UNDER VARIOUS MARKET CONDITIONS

Now that we are familiar with the five funds entered in the competition, let's have some market action so that we can compare their performance records. (Refer to Table 1 as often as it may be necessary to follow the text.)

Market movement number 1

RISE OF 30 PERCENT. The first market movement we have hypothecated is a rise of 30 percent in the general market (or, more realistically, perhaps, the group of stocks traded by our theoretical funds, which might well tend to be subject to wider swings than the general market). For the moment, let's not be concerned about the time period involved; this will be considered later.

Because of the 30 percent rise, the Cash Fund, which is invested 100 percent long, of course gains 30. The Mutual Fund, which is only 70 percent long, gains only 21, while its 30 percent in cash lies idle. In these illustrations we are ignoring interest earned or paid, dividends, brokerage fees, taxes, etc. Only theoretical capital gains and losses need concern us here.

As a result of the market rise, all three Hedge Funds make a profit on their longs but lose on their shorts. The net gain for all three Hedge Funds, no matter how leveraged, is constant at 21—the same as the gain of the Mutual Fund. This illustration begins to give a feel for the effect of the "risk." With or without leverage, and no matter what the amount of leverage may be, the funds with equal "risk" will show exactly the same gain.

Thus, at the end of the first round, the Cash Fund is ahead with a gain of 30, while the other four funds are exactly tied, all with a gain of 21. (The hedge funder might comment at this point that the Cash Fund won only because of its higher "risk.")

Market movement number 2

THE MARKET DROPS 30 PERCENT. This is bad news for everyone, but such drops do occur. How are the various funds affected? Let's ignore for the time being the protective measures that might have been taken, for there is something to be learned about fund behavior in this simple market movement.

The results, as we would expect, are exactly the reverse of those in the foregoing 30 percent market rise. The Cash Fund loses 30, the Mutual Fund and the Hedge Funds all lose 21. All of the last four funds were hedged, but not enough to avoid net losses. Nevertheless, the hedges did provide *some* protection, even in a major bear movement. Note that the "risk" concept seems to be working well. *All the hedged funds suf-*

fered exactly the same loss—even though leveraging is ordi- narily considered very risky, with risk (no quotation marks) increasing in direct proportion to the amount of leverage. (Risk and "risk" will be considered in detail in Section 3.)

Note also that no adjustment in the "risk" is made even in this bear market. The object of this table is to show how the funds would perform with *constant* "risk."

Market movement number 3

IN A GENERALLY RISING MARKET THE HEDGE FUNDS' LONGS GO UP MORE THAN THE SHORTS: 40 PERCENT AND 10 PERCENT RE- SPECTIVELY. This is one of the situations in which hedge funds are supposed to outperform the general market, even if their shorts go up. Let's compare, then, the performance of our various funds, supposing—as we do in all these examples— equal competence of fund managers in buying and selling stocks.

All three Hedge Funds, as shown in Table 1, beat the Mutual Fund, and the higher the leverage the better the per- formance. The 100% Hedge Fund clears a net profit of 47.5— *appreciably higher than the rise of 40 percent by the longs as a group, even though a loss was taken on the shorts.*

The Cash Fund equals the gain of the 50% Hedge Fund (but of course with a higher "risk" than the hedge fund).

Market movement number 4

IN A GENERALLY FALLING MARKET THE LONGS DROP 10 PERCENT, THE HEDGERS' SHORTS 40 PERCENT. This is another situation in which superior performance is claimed for the hedge funds, and Table 1 supports this claim. While all other funds show a *loss,* the leveraged hedge funds show a *gain,* and the higher the leverage, the greater the gain.

Market movement number 5

THE HEDGERS' DREAMS COME TRUE! THEIR LONGS GO UP, THEIR SHORTS GO DOWN, EACH BY 30 PERCENT. The 100% Hedge Fund is the winner, with a gain of 60, followed by the 45 gain of the 50% Hedge Fund—pointing up once again the effect of leverage. The Cash Hedge Fund does no better than the Cash Fund, however, and both are trailed by the Mutual Fund.

SUMMARY OF RESULTS

In order to make an overall comparison of the performance of our five funds, let's suppose that the five market movements described did in fact occur. What then is the average gain for each fund? The results, in the next-to-last line of Table 1, show the clear superiority of the leveraged hedge funds. The 100% Hedge Fund has an average gain of 24 percent, double that of the Cash Fund, and nearly three times that of the Mutual Fund. The bottom line of Table 1 shows what the "cumulative" returns would be if the five market movements occurred in any order, each movement starting with $100 paid-in capital. (Here cumulative is used to mean simply that the five results are added in each case. If each event started with the gains or losses of the previous movement applied to paid-in capital, the leveraged hedge funds would do even better.)

The 100% Hedge Fund in Table 1 shows a resounding 120 percent cumulative gain, again double that of the Cash Fund, and nearly three times that of the Mutual Fund. The 50% Hedge Fund gains 90 percent on its paid-in capital, and the Cash Hedge Fund 60 percent.

Even if the five-event cycle covered a time span of three years, the average annual gain of the 100% Hedge Fund would be 40 percent.

Note also that all of the cumulative results would be exactly the same if only the last three market events had taken place, since the first two cancel each other. If such a three-event cycle occurred in, say, 18 months, the average annual gain by the 100% Hedge Fund would be 80 percent.

The *average* gains in the three-event cycle of course would be one third of the cumulative gain in each case, that is, 40 percent for the 100% Hedge Fund, 30 percent for the 50% Hedge Fund, and 20 percent for the Cash and Cash Hedge Funds. The Mutual Fund, with 14 percent, comes in last.

The figures for average returns also represent what the statistical analyst calls *expected values*. In other words, the cycle of events need not take place at all. If the individual events have *equal probabilities of occurrence,* the investor can *expect* a gain equal to the average shown, no matter what happens in any event. What this means is that he may get more, he may get less, but he will probably get the same gain as the average indicated for each case.

The five market movements we have hypothecated will not, of course, happen so neatly in the real world. It is more realistic to think of them as averages. In a generally rising market, for example, every stock in the portfolio will not go up exactly 30 percent. A few of the longs may double in price, a few may be losers, and most will be somewhere in between. The end result, however, could in fact be a 30 percent increase in the total amount invested long. The same kind of reasoning applies to the other market movements.

It is also true, of course, that market actions of the types hypothecated could all be taking place simultaneously in a single portfolio containing several individual stocks. And the faster the individual favorable events take place, the greater will be the annual return, or capital gain, on paid-in capital.

We have elaborated on Table 1 much more than our young hedge funder did at the blackboard. If the discussion about expected values and probabilities has clouded the issue for any reader, he should return for a moment to Table 1 to renew his faith in leveraged hedge funds.

The importance of hedging vs. leverage

In the preceding pages the reader—if he was not too dazzled by the performance of the leveraged hedge funds—may have noticed that the Cash Fund, which was fully invested long throughout the various market events, came out with exactly the same average and cumulative results as the Cash Hedge Fund, which hedged its position by going 85 percent long and 15 percent short.

This raises the question: Was the superior performance of the leveraged hedge funds due solely to leverage?

In order to answer this question, let's set up a Leverage Fund, using 50 percent leverage and investing only long, and compare its performance to that of the 50% Hedge Fund with which we are already familiar.

Table 2 shows the results obtained by the two funds under exactly the same market conditions described for Table 1. Fund D, the 50% Hedge Fund, of course shows exactly the same results as before. Fund F, the new Leverage Fund, out-performs the equally leveraged hedge fund in market movements 1 and 3, does worse in 2 and 4, and does just as well in number 5.

The overall results for average return and cumulative return are *exactly the same* for the two funds, *despite the fact that four of the five market actions are types which supposedly favor superior performance by a hedge fund.*

TABLE 2

Hedge fund and leverage fund performance
under various market conditions
($100 paid-in capital; 50 percent leverage)

	50% Hedge Fund (D)	50% Leverage Fund (F)
Invested long	110	150
Invested short	40	
"Risk"	70	150
1. Longs up 30%	+33	+45
Shorts up 30%	−12	
Net change	+21	+45
2. Longs down 30%	−33	−45
Shorts down 30%	+12	
Net change	−21	−45
3. Longs up 40%	+44	+60
Shorts up 10%	− 4	
Net change	+40	+60
4. Longs down 10%	−11	−15
Shorts down 40%	+16	
Net change	+ 5	−15
5. Longs up 30%	+33	+45
Shorts down 30% ....+12		
Net change .... +45		+45
Average return %	18	18
Cumulative return %	90	90

From this, we must conclude that *there is no inherent magic in merely being hedged.* A hedge fund with a constant "risk," as in our examples so far, will perform better in some markets than an equally leveraged fund invested all long; in other markets it will perform worse. In the long run, such hedging takes away as much as it gives.

This conclusion is rather disappointing, but it will lead to a clearer understanding of the real reasons (*including hedging*) for the hedge funds' superior potential.

section THREE

Hedge fund techniques used, abused, and improved

The real reasons for the superior potential of hedge funds

LEVERAGE

THE ABILITY to magnify results by using leverage is one of the most important reasons that hedge funds can outperform other types of investment vehicles.

The manager of a conventional mutual fund which has, say, $10 million in capital cannot—even if he stays fully invested—equal the performance of the manager of a leveraged fund who borrows to increase his invested funds from $10 million to $15 million, given equal ability to make profitable stock selections. Even if he selects the *same* stocks, he can make only two thirds the gain of the leveraged fund.

Of course, we knew it all the time, didn't we? But it does seem to take a little luster off the comparisons that *Fortune* and *Business Week* made between the relative performance of Jones' hedge funds and the Fidelity Trend and Dreyfus mutual funds. It's really not fair to compare them. It's not fair because it is not a real comparison of the fund managers' abilities in stock selection and timing. The Mutual Fund of Table 1 cannot match the performance of the 50% or 100% Hedge Funds. The striking differences in that example, as we have seen, lie in leverage.

Section Four of this book is devoted to the important subject of leverage.

STOCK SELECTION AND TIMING

Up until now, in comparing the various types of funds, we have assumed equal competence of the funds' managers in stock selection and timing. In other words, we have kept that factor constant in order to study the effect of other variables: leverage, market movements, and short selling.

However, stock selection (with its ever-related timing) is the biggest variable of all those affecting performance. The leverage factor, it is true, can easily affect a fund's performance by 50 or 100 percent, but superior stock selection can result in well over 100 percent annual appreciation, while poor selection can result in a loss. That's a real variable.

The *most* important factor in hedge fund performance is stock selection and timing. Prosaic as the fact may seem to most of us, we cannot escape it, even with the hedge fund formula. We'll have more to say on stock selection and timing in the discussion following this.

At this point, the reader might well say: Okay, so stock selection and leverage are very important factors in hedge fund performance. But what about the concept of hedging itself? And short selling? And "risk"? Do they help at all?

SHORT SELLING

Short selling will be discussed in detail later in this section. The short answer on short selling, however, is intuitive: Stocks go down as well as up, so doesn't it make good sense to place part of the bets that way? Especially in a bear market, where by definition more stocks are going down than up, the simple probability of picking a winning short over a winning long is evident.

HEDGING: ADJUSTING THE LONG/SHORT RATIO

The answer on hedging is that *it does* moderate the effect of sudden or unexpected market swings on the portfolio; *it does* permit taking advantage of good shorts as well as good longs; and *it does* permit full and profitable investment of funds during bear markets as well as bull.

Also, the hedge concept does allow the fund manager time in which he can profitably adjust the "risk," or proportion of longs and shorts in his portfolio, to take account of changing conditions.

In Tables 1 and 2, the "risk" during all market movements remained constant at 70 percent. In practice, however, the fund manager would adjust the proportion of longs and shorts in an effort to keep in tune with unfolding events.

Let's examine how the 50% Hedge Fund might perform with such adjustments. We can't expect perfect response from the fund manager, but let's allow him at least to roll a little with the punches.

Table 3 hypothecates the same five market movements used in Tables 1 and 2. In bull markets, represented by events 1 and 3, the "risk" that would produce the highest profits would be 100 percent, that is, 100 percent of funds invested long. Let's assume that the manager decides on only 80 percent. His performance, of course, improves over what it was with 70 percent "risk." In these two bull movements, he still does not do as well as the 50% Leverage Fund, whose results are also repeated, for comparison, in Table 3.

In the bear markets—events 2 and 4—the manager decides on a "risk" of *minus* 70 percent, that is, 40 long and 110 short. As a result of his adjustment of longs and shorts, the manager will gain 21 in event 2 instead of losing that amount, and in event 4 he will gain 40 instead of 5. Of course, the Leverage Fund loses heavily in both movements.

If event 5 is a sideways movement, the manager decides on zero "risk," investing 75 long and 75 short. In this case his gain, 45, remains the same as with 70 percent "risk," because both the longs and the shorts move 30 percent in the desired directions.

However, the four improvements noted raise his overall return average from 18 to 34.5 percent, and his cumulative return from 90 to 172.5 percent.

Table 3 illustrates how a capable hedge fund manager, by

TABLE 3
Hedge fund performance with adjusted "risk"
($100 paid-in capital; 50 percent leverage)

	50% Hedge Fund (Adjusted Risk)	50% Hedge Fund (70% Risk)	50% Leverage Fund (100% Long)
1. "Risk" 80%			
Longs (115) up 30% .... + 34.5			
Shorts (35) up 30% .... − 10.5			
Net change .... + 24	+21	+45
2. "Risk" minus 70%			
Longs (40) down 30% ...... − 12			
Shorts (110) down 30% ..... + 33			
Net change .... + 21	−21	−45
3. "Risk" 80%			
Longs (115) up 40% .... + 46			
Shorts (35) up 10% .... − 3.5			
Net change .... + 42.5	+40	+60
4. "Risk" minus 70%			
Longs (40) down 10% ...... − 4			
Shorts (110) down 40% ..... + 44			
Net change ....+ 40	+ 5	−15
5. "Risk" zero			
Longs (75) up 30% .... + 22.5			
Shorts (75) down 30% ...... + 22.5			
Net change .... + 45	+45	+45
Average return % .... + 34.5	+18	+18
Cumulative return % .... +172.5	+90	+90

adjusting his longs and shorts to remain *only roughly in tune* with the prevailing market trends, can nearly double the performance realized by both constant-"risk" and equally leveraged funds.

While there is no magic at all in a hedged position that remains constant, *the results gained by adjusting the "risk" can be phenomenal.* Adjusting the "risk," of course, is still essentially a matter of stock selection and timing, but hedging permits a wider and more profitable field for their use.

A simple method for adjusting the longs and shorts to keep in tune with the market is suggested in a later discussion, which also considers the subject of hedging in more detail.

Selection and timing

SOURCES OF INFORMATION AND ASSISTANCE

THIS CHAPTER, on the crucial business of selection and timing, would appear to be the easiest one to write, because the area has already been given so much attention by others. Hopefully, it could be put in a single sentence: Get yourself a good stock advisory service, or a good broker, or both.

Certainly these services are offered in abundance, and for them the investing public pays, in one way or another, a great many millions of dollars every year. There are about a half-dozen stock analysts for every stock listed on the Big Board. Brokers are even more numerous, and their firms spew out recommendations by the megaream. The pages of financial publications overflow with columns of data and advice, and their ad pages beckon with promises of diverse paths to the True Grail.

This avalanche of advice is not matched, unfortunately, by a counterflow of testimonial letters praising its effectiveness. How often do we write, or even hear about, anything along the following lines?

> DEAR SIR:
>
> The undersigned has been a client of yours for ___ years. Over this time I have developed great confidence in your recommendations and base my investment decisions on your advice. As a result, although I began with modest means, I am now independently wealthy.

I suppose you hear this from your other clients all
the time, but I simply had to express my gratitude.
Yours very sincerely,

One man who did get rich, not by taking advice but by selling it, is Arnold Bernhard, the founder, owner, and boss of
Value Line Investment Survey, which is reported to have
made him "several times a millionaire." His trademark is the
Greek Temple of Reason, and his stock ratings are based on
a formula designed to reveal each stock's true value: that of
its future dividends discounted back to the present.

"By sticking to Bernhard's principles," reported *Forbes*
(October 1, 1969), "Value Line has been pretty consistently
wrong about the stock market since the mid-Fifties." (But it
is, "statistically speaking, a darned good service.") Starting
in 1950, Bernhard got into the mutual fund business. Value
Line Fund and later Value Line Income Fund, both using his
principles, did not "set the world on fire," according to *Forbes*,
but the Value Line Special Situations Fund, which "parted
company with [Value Line's] basic principles" and resorted
to the go-go devices of the performance game was a big success—for a while, at least (but it was sorely hit by the 1969-70
bear market).

Speaking of principles, the former editor of another investment advisory service (*Indicator Digest* and *Technical Stock
Reports*) was recently dealt with rather sternly by the SEC
for following, himself, the very same advice that he was selling to his customers. (See the *Wall Street Journal*, October
27, 1969.) The SEC's objections, it seems, were based on his
timing (and we know how important timing is); the Commission charged that he was buying "for the accounts of certain
persons" just before publication, and selling soon after the
publicity pushed up the stock price of the issues praised. His
brokers were also chastised by the SEC for their alleged part
in the affair. (Respondents consented to the findings without
admitting to the allegations.)

This incident may indicate that brokers are at least willing
to help, in whatever way they can. (But we can't always count
on this degree of cooperation from our own account executive;

it appears that the "former editor" and the brokerage sales-man involved are brothers.)

To be fair, there are brokers who do a good job. The trouble is that we expect too much of them. They are, after all, sales-men and, even as the salesmen of vacuum cleaners, they must sell their products in order to get their commissions. Of course, if what they sell us enables us to clean up, they're de-lighted; that's good for future sales.

Commissions help to support not only the salesman that the ordinary investor deals with, but also his superiors in the upper hierarchy of the firm, including those who may be supplementing their incomes—"moonlighting" is not quite the right term—by participation in underwriting stock issues, or even running private hedge funds.

Even supposing that these higher talents were made di-rectly available to the ordinary investor, his financial success would be by no means assured. Consider the words of one analyst and hedge fund manager writing in the *Financial Analysts Journal*:[3] "The talent for grasping the full dimen-sions of an unfolding story is rarely found on the floor of the New York Stock Exchange or even in the ken of the most thorough industry specialist."

Well, then, how about turning to the people who actually manage portfolios? Another writer in the same issue of the *Financial Analysts Journal* has this discouraging word: "Many portfolio managers know little about their own de-cision-making process and even less about their methods of reviewing accounts."

The above examples have not been cited in order to shake the reader's confidence in The American Way of Life, but rather to encourage him to place the various sources of infor-mation and assistance in a rational perspective, and to give him confidence that in using his own abilities and judgment in managing his funds he will not be facing insuperable com-petition. It's superable.

INVESTMENT APPROACHES

Even the shrewdest managers of the private hedge funds have problems, it should comfort us to know. Barton Biggs, of

$30 million Fairfield Partners told *Barron's*:[11] "We've tried very hard to find a service or a technique that is going to lead us into the promised land, but they always seem to let you down in the clutch. I think you just have to rely on your instincts, and your instincts are wrong a lot of the time."

On the other hand, the reliance on instincts is not complete: "We just try to do a thorough analytical job, then go long the best stocks and short the worst."

Analysis, to a fund manager, can cover a wide range of activities. Some swear loyalty to the fundamentalist approach; that is, digging out the facts on such matters as a company's net worth, past and projected earnings, debt structure, current and numerous other ratios, quality of management, and so on; and how all these are related to the larger fundamentals of the company's position in the industry, industry trends, and economic factors such as spendable income, interest rates, money supply, and growth of the gross national product. The fundamentalists' bible is that excellent tome, *Security Analysis*, by Graham and Dodd (joined by Cottle in the latest edition).

The so-called technicians, or technical analysts, on the other hand, say, in effect: Sure, we admit all these things can affect stock prices, but there are too many variables; it's impossible for anyone to know all the answers, and a single misjudged or entirely unforeseen factor can throw your whole fundamental assessment out of line.

All factors meet in the market, continues the technician, and are there reflected in supply and demand, which in fact determine stock prices and price movements.

Charts provide a record of the interplay of supply and demand, an easily read summary of the price changes and trading volumes that have taken place in a stock or in a group of stocks, such as the Dow Jones Industrials. Price movements often tend to fall into a number of chart patterns, or "formations," and from them the analyst judges relationships between buying and selling pressures.

Although there is no infallible system for predicting stock prices, admits the technician, history does often repeat itself

in the stock market, so charts can be used to determine the
relative strength of supply and demand at various price levels,
and therefore to predict the probable direction and extent of
price movements.

The chartists and their critics really split on the ability to
predict. Protagonists of the delightfully named "random
walk" theory, while conceding that supply and demand are
reflected in market prices, maintain that overadjustments,
underadjustments, lags and advance movements will result
in a "random walk market," in which successive price changes
are independent. In short, past prices are not a reliable indication of what future prices will be.

To illustrate by oversimplification: If a flipped coin comes
up heads 10 times straight, has it set a reliable trend? No; the
probability of heads is still 50-50 on the next toss. A member
of Congress, during hearings not long ago on mutual fund
management fees, further illustrated the random walk theory
by using the dart-board approach to stock selection—with, he
maintained, results comparable to those of professional management.

Must we conclude, then, that fundamental and technical
analysis, both of which are used extensively by money managers, including those of the private and public hedge funds,
are a waste of time?

Not entirely. Fundamentals are still the most important
determinants of price changes, especially over the longer
term, even though sneak factors often creep in to frustrate the
orderly realization of the soundest predictions. Nor has the
law of supply and demand been repealed. Charts do provide
a convenient summary of a stock's history, and they can be
useful if deification of the trickier nuances is avoided, and if
it is remembered that stock charts are no more "technical"
than charts of fevers or emotions—which in fact they are.
Trends must end, it is true, but the law of inertia hasn't been
repealed either; even the most pure fundamentalist might
help his timing by glancing, however surreptitiously, at a
stock chart.

For the hedge funder, velocity ratings can be judged

quickly from a chart without resorting to tedious calculations.

Some common ground can almost be discerned between the chartists and the random walkers. The technicians say that history *often* repeats itself; the random walkers say that history is not a *reliable* guide to the future.

In investment approaches, hedge fund managers run the gamut, ranging from almost religious fundamentalism, through charting and technical analysis, even through "instinctive" decision making, to—we have it on good authority, straight from a hedge fund manager—"coat-tailing," or jumping on stocks that the manager hears other managers are jumping on.

COMPUTERS AND THE LEMMING SYNDROME

In the coat-tailing operation, computers can be a great help, as we shall see in a moment. Computers are already very useful in stock analysis; they can store vast amounts of information, screen that information, and provide quick answers (to the question, for example: which companies have at least $100 million annual sales, 15 percent rate of growth over X years, Y capitalization, Z debt structure; you name it?). The computer can come up with the list in a trice, because all the necessary data have been fed into it previously. However, when it comes to predicting the future, the computer rates somewhere behind your pet schnauzer (who presumably is alert enough to sense when his dinner is on the way).

What the computer can do is alert its master to *current* market price changes (of any designated magnitude or pattern) accompanied by a designated up or down volume (keyed to number of shares, percentage of stock outstanding, or whatever). Thus alerted, the fund manager who is nimble enough (he probably hasn't time to analyze *why* the stock is moving up or down) joins the movement, going long on the boomers and short on the sickies. Of course, every other gunslinger with his own computer or a sharp eye on the ticker tape is doing about the same thing. The added volume pushes the price still higher (in the case of an up movement), confirming their predictions and fulfilling their most sanguine expectations. Of course, the noncomputerized public, also affected by the Lemming Syndrome, is getting its share of the action. Zuccini-Lox Leasing up another 9 today! Buy more!

The run-up, interrupted perhaps by a few gut-wrenching reversals, goes on. At some point, the computer barks a warning: X price slippage on Y volume—time to take profits! The Xs and Ys set by the masters are not all quite the same, but the warnings all sound about the same time. Now the Lemming Syndrome is operating in reverse. Some sales are made in time to clear a profit, or even sell short, but the inrush of sell orders accelerates the price decline, and the bids dry up. A lot of investors who joined the mad rush, like the unfortunate lemmings, go over the cliff. The fund manager affected by the Lemming Syndrome explains that he happened to get whip-sawed, and calls for a more sophisticated attitude from his agitated investors.

Do you remember Bernie Cornfeld's man in Maryland? Well, *he* has a computer, a Control Data 3600, which he uses to study price and volume patterns and trends in order to spot glamour stocks, which he defines simply as stocks that are *moving. Forbes*[19] remarked on the fact that "so many of the computer-powered managers come up with the same answers." The reply: It is necessary to "come up with new ways to play the computer game" and to develop "newer and better portfolio strategies—like the glamour stock index . . . As soon as you get a new technique everyone else gets it, and it's necessary to develop still newer techniques."

This game is not recommended for the general reader, even if he happens to have a computer. The number of hedge fund managers playing is not known.

DIVERSITY OF APPROACHES

Most fund managers use a more fundamental approach, or combine fundamentals with technical analysis. "We've made our big money from basic trends," Mr. Biggs told *Barron's*.

Barron's[25, 26] also interviewed Leo Goldner, a general partner in Mount Vernon Associates, a $5 million hedge fund. Mr. Goldner, who may represent the golden mean of hedge fund managers, said that the majority of his ideas "come from people in the brokerage business," but "We still do a lot of homework. We attempt to cross check every idea with two or three sources. We contact the broker or analysts who follow the situation. We plot most of the stocks we follow, and we often get in touch with the companies themselves. We can't do the type of in-depth research we used to, but we can touch base with the companies to make sure they exist."

Mr. Goldner added a few well-chosen words on the role of the hedge fund manager: "The really crucial point of all this is the fact that we've had ten years in the business. Rather than paying us to go out and dig the ditches, people are now paying us to supervise the work and to reflect on ways to dig bigger and better ditches." The reader is challenged to come up with a more apt figure of speech.

Aside from their various approaches to stock analysis, hedge fund managers show a diversity in other basics as well. Most managers severely limit the number of stocks in their portfolios, while some (the Old Master among them) believe in diversification as a means of spreading the risk. Many believe in short-term trading; others, including most of the fundamentalists, believe in investing for the longer pull. They are all alike in one respect: their investment goal is capital gains, preferably long term; dividends are virtually ignored.

1929 AND ALL THAT

John Kenneth Galbraith, writing recently in *Harper's*,[33] indicates that he had at least some hedge fund managers in mind when he reminded us that "financial genius consists almost entirely of a well-developed capacity for self-delusion combined with a rising market."

The article was written in celebration of the 40th anniversary of the Great Crash of 1929, about which Mr. Galbraith has written a most readable and sobering book. By some, he is considered almost a proponent of another Great Crash. This judgment is probably too harsh. Still, in another book, he did succeed in giving affluence a bad name.

On the constructive side, it is worthwhile for the ordinary investor, especially in bull markets which have boomed along for some time, to restore a sober point of view by certain remedial readings or re-readings. Suggestions: *Extraordinary Popular Delusions and the Madness of Crowds,* written by Charles Mackay in 1841, and still fresh; *The Money Game,* written recently under the pseudonym of "Adam Smith," and very fresh; and almost anything by John Kenneth Galbraith.

Another aid in restoring a proper scepticism level in over-ebullient investors is reading the *Barron's* feature "Up and Down Wall Street," which some people whose companies are analyzed therein might prefer to call "Up and Down the Wall," which is where it drives them.

TIPS FROM ALL OVER

Although such reading may help to imbue in the investor a common-sense outlook toward the market in general, it is not of much help in the selection and timing of specific issues. However, some help might be found in that old saw, "Cut your losses, and let your profits ride." Like most old saws, it could use some hedging.

"Cut your losses," certainly. We don't *have* to sit still while our investments depreciate 30 or 50 percent or more. At the time we take any position, long or short, in any stock, we can resolve right then that if events prove to us that we have guessed wrong, the maximum loss we will take is, say, 10 percent. Accepting a loss takes courage, because we must admit that we have been fools. But only *little,* or 10 percent, fools. Not the big fools we'd be after a 50 percent drop. Consider how the performance records of *all* the funds in Tables 1, 2, and 3 would have been improved simply by using stop-loss orders in the various market situations.

But human nature being what it is, we find it easier to procrastinate, in the hope that a reversal will vindicate our ordinarily flawless judgment. A turnaround may come, but it is more likely that the slide will go on, and on, and on.

How many times have we said to ourselves, as we watched

our soundly chosen stock drop lower and lower, *"How much lower can it go?"* As a possible aid in such situations, the author offers a bad couplet—bad enough, he hopes, to pop unbidden into the consciousness at the first sickening price drop:

> Ask not how low your stock can go,
> You know damn' well it's near zer-O!

With the accent on the last, or wrong, syl-*lab*-le.

So much for cutting losses. How about letting the profits ride? We've all had the experience of letting them ride *too* long, right up and over the old roller coaster. When *should* we sell? We don't want to be pigs, of course; we've heard that other old Wall Street saw about bulls and bears making money, but pigs never. Still, we'd like to do at least as well as Baron Rothschild, who reportedly uttered that famous line about owing his success to always selling *too soon*. (Just as an aside, *all* the Rothschilds seem to be Barons; the author knows one Baron Rothschild who frequents a bar in the West Fifties.)

But what's a pig, and what's too soon? It is virtually impossible to set the right percentage gain. With some stocks, a 10 percent gain taken after a quick move is in order; other stocks double and triple and more. Just what is the dividing line between socially acceptable avarice and porcine greed? Alas! there is no rule to guide us.

For what it may be worth, we offer—as a sell signal on your good actors—the Euphoria Index: When you feel so good about a stock that you don't know how you could feel any better, you couldn't. Sell!

SUMMARY AND CONCLUSION

To sum up, it has not been the purpose of this discussion to deride all sources of information and assistance in the important and necessary matter of stock selection and timing, but rather to instill a healthy attitude of scepticism (which lies somewhere between cynicism and credulity) in their use.

A good broker is hard, but not impossible, to find; just remember that he probably has less time to read the *Wall Street Journal* than you have yourself. Much helpful information can be found, certainly, in publications such as *Barron's, Fortune, Financial Analysts Journal, Forbes,* and the *Wall Street Journal,* but the tendency to take everything literally that happens to have numbers in it should be overcome. The authors are often trying to tell us some very enlightening and even amusing things, although editorial policy doesn't permit them to set it to music. *Barron's* "Talking Money" feature, wherein money managers of various stripes do most of the talking, is quite instructive. You may even find there a money manager's style that fits your own investment philosophy.

Another type of investment reading consists of registration statements, prospectuses and proxy material, which often contain many useful facts about individual companies. Of course, these are written or edited by lawyers, so they are not really meant to be understood by the ordinary investor. Nevertheless, it is often possible to dig out facts about a company which would never appear in its annual report or other inspirational literature. In both prospectuses and annual reports, some of the most interesting facts can be found in the footnotes. As a general rule, the magnitude of the bad news varies inversely with the size of the print, and directly with the compounding of negatives.

Balance sheets and income statements can also be useful sources of information, especially if the reader has some aptitude for accounting and an interest in shifting depreciation methods, creative income and reserve manipulation, and imaginative pooling of interest techniques. The Accounting Principles Board of the AICPA (American Institute of Certified Public Accountants) is trying to bring some standardization to these areas, but there is quite naturally a lot of opposition, even within the board itself, it would appear.

Finally, many basic facts about companies are available in the publications of Moody's and Standard & Poor's, but even

Short selling

THE SIMPLE SIDE OF SELLING SHORT

A SHORT SALE is made in the expectation that the price of the stock will decline. For example, 100 shares of Pat-A-Kake Franchise Systems is sold short at 50. If the stock declines to 40 and is bought or "covered" at that price, the profit is $1,000 (less the usual brokerage fees and transfer tax). If the price goes up to 60 and the short sale is covered there, a loss of $1,000 results.

The short seller must, sooner or later, complete the transaction by buying the same number of shares he sold short.

Short sales can be made only on the "uptick" or the "zero-plus" tick. In other words, the price at which the short sale is made must be at least one-eighth of a point higher (the uptick) than the preceding transaction in that stock, or at the same price as the preceding transaction (zero-plus tick) if *that* was higher than the preceding different price. This rule was designed to moderate the depressing effect that short selling might otherwise have on a declining stock.

These are the simple facts about selling short—that critical and essential ingredient of hedge fund operation. Let's proceed to the complications.

THE DARK SIDE OF THE MARKET

Short selling has been called "the dark side of the market,"[5] and even worse. Many people seem to feel instinctively that short selling is the embodiment of evil. Even our government discriminates against it. The SEC, with its uptick rule, tries to restrain short selling; and even if a profit is made, it is subjected to harsher tax treatment than long-term gains made by buying long.

No objections are raised if a profit is made by buying a stock and selling it later. This is considered normal, constructive, and fully in accord with the Protestant, Judeo-Christian, and any other known ethic.

However, if these two simple actions—buying and selling—are done in reverse order, which is all that short selling amounts to, attitudes undergo a profound change. This is sinister, destructive, unethical and—apparently—un-American, in the view of at least two official agencies of the U.S. government.

Most of the objection to short selling appears to be a hold-over from the era of the Robber Barons, based on subliminal memories of the ruthless bear raids of such bad guys as Jim Fisk, Jay Gould and Dan Drew. But in a later and even more disastrous era, that of the Great Crash, Joseph P. Kennedy added to his already large assets by selling short. This was before the uptick rule was conceived to moderate bear markets, when short selling could accelerate price drops. However, apparently not enough stigma was attached to Mr. Kennedy's bear market activities to prevent his appointment as first head of the SEC, an agency formed by the then new Roosevelt administration to crack down on the bad guys of Wall Street; nor has public indignation been evidenced by refusal to elect three of Mr. Kennedy's sons to high office.

Still, the prejudice against short selling itself lingers on. Even the most up-to-date business school types who are running some if not most of the hedge funds are distinctly uncomfortable in handling the short selling side of the business. One told the *Wall Street Journal*:[21] "I'm always looking for good short sales . . . but I'd rather be a bull. I don't enjoy this [1969 bear] market at all. It hurts my stomach."

Indeed, the sorry performances reported in the *Journal*

article appear to reflect an almost masochistic attitude toward short selling among some hedge fund managers; they seem to be asking for punishment.

Through good markets and bad, there is a striking unanimity about the difficulties of short selling. Hedge fund managers, even including the Old Master, according to *Fortune*, "normally consider themselves lucky to break even on their short portfolios."

"If anything, shorting has held us back," one manager told *Barron's*.[11] "You never make any real money on shorts. All you do is try to preserve your money in a down market." Moreover, "nobody's terribly good at it."[12] Some other hedge fund managers seem more concerned with getting a good night's rest than with making money on their shorts. "It is always preferable to pick a short you can sleep with,"[4] advises one, and another says of the hedge concept, "I need it to sleep nights."[1] But judging by the general unease, abdominal distress and other symptoms afflicting hedge fund managers, not many of their shorts make good sleeping companions.

A somewhat less fatalistic view is expressed by fund managers who seem to rationalize their unprofitable short investments by claiming that their shorts allow a more "aggressive" stance on the long side of the market. What this means is that all losses and gains on short positions, no matter how long held, are treated as short term for tax purposes, so they can be used to offset short-term gains and losses on the long side without regard to the holding period. It also means, apparently, that because of his short position the fund manager feels he is to some extent hedged against market vicissitudes and is therefore free to take greater risks on the long side.

Short selling, says the *New York Times*,[5] "is no game for the faint of heart, the financially weak, or the neophyte." This judgment, if true, would seem to eliminate most of us, but we can take some cheer from the foregoing examples, which indicate that short selling is no game either for the weak of stomach, the financially strong, or the professionals—which would seem to make it unanimous.

THE BRIGHTER SIDE OF SELLING SHORT

It would be appropriate to exorcise at least some of the
devils who seem to have taken over the nether world of short
selling. We might even discover that some of the spirits-in-
residence are benevolent.

Putting prejudice aside for a moment, let's consider some
fundamentals. Markets go up; markets go down. You needn't
go back as far as 1929, with Mr. Galbraith, to know that
markets go down. You know markets go down if you reached
an age of awareness before 1962, or even 1966—and that
should include almost all of you, with the possible exception
of a few of the youngest hedge fund managers. For them, we
had 1969.

Not only do markets go down, but the prices of individual
stocks go down, often even in upside markets. Every market
day, no matter what the overall trend, records its declines as
well as its advances, its downside as well as its upside volume,
and usually new lows as well as new highs.

That being so, everyone should have the inalienable, un-
fettered right to believe that a stock will, on occasion, go down
—and the right to risk his own money to back that opinion.
There should be no more restriction on selling short than on
buying long. Both involve a purchase and a sale; only the
timing is different. To handicap short selling is much like
saying that it's all right to bet your money for the football
team you think is going to win, but you mustn't bet against a
team you think will lose.

The uptick rule, by hampering short selling, does perhaps
serve a useful purpose by moderating downside markets, but
a "downtick" rule—which not even the SEC has proposed—
would make much more sense during runaway upside moves,
which have caught a lot more people and cost them a great
deal more money than can ever be blamed on short selling.

Is it immoral or sinister to sell a stock with the expectation
that its price will go down to some point where one can buy it
and show a profit? Hardly. The short seller believes that the

price of a particular stock will decline, and he may even be hoping and praying that it will do so, but he is not praying for the collapse of the whole economy. Generally speaking, his morality could probably be compared favorably with that of an administration which uses government powers to tighten the financial screws on everybody in order to "cool the economy." Besides, the hedger has his longs as well as his shorts to worry about; he's not praying for universal disaster.

Before we leave the subject of public morality and the common weal, let's ask: Why shouldn't a part of the citizenry (the short sellers) be happy and making money even during bear markets? Must we all be depressed at the same time?

Even the most practical of economic considerations would seem to demand a substantial short position in the stock market. Think how all the curves of the economic indicators would be smoothed out if half, say, of all investors were making profits during bear markets!

A high short position, furthermore, represents future demand, and therefore gives strong support to the market itself.

There is an additional important function that active short selling performs: it lends liquidity to the market by helping to satisfy demand, which is, after all, what a free market is all about. A short seller, be it remembered, is not forcing his stock on the buyer. The buyer believes that the stock is going up, and he might well be right.

BIAS AGAINST SELLING SHORT

Given above are some of the reasons why short selling *should* be given the same consideration and treatment as buying long. In practice, of course, it is not. The uptick rule is applied to short selling; there is no downtick rule for buying long. All capital gains made by selling short, even if the position is held more than six months, are taxed as regular income; profits on long positions held over six months, are taxed as long-term gains, with a top rate of 25 percent.

There is not much the investor can do about the uptick rule, although it does not apply to unlisted stocks, and the

Pacific Coast Stock Exchange, for one, does not enforce it for odd-lot, i.e., up to 99-share, short sales of listed stocks. The investor can attempt to overcome the effect of higher taxes on short selling by more frequent turnover, since there is no inducement to hold on for long-term gains. This tactic is favored by the fact that declines often take place over a shorter time span than the equivalent upswings. Long-term tax treatment for a short position *can* be obtained by purchasing a put option, holding it over six months, and selling it before the exercise date. (Puts and calls are discussed in Section Four.)

It is not easy to explain completely the government prejudice against selling short. "The SEC *doesn't understand* short selling," one hedge fund manager told the author. He could be right; he got to know the SEC quite well during discussions over the content of his fund's prospectus, so his opinion had the ring of authority.

The general prejudice against short selling could be based in part on the risk involved. To counter all risk charges, the hedge funders have a neat riposte; they say, "By hedging our positions, we are using speculative techniques for conservative ends." The conservative aspect, however, is not a conspicuous feature in the prospectuses of the public hedge funds; risk is.

The risk story that is used to frighten would-be short sellers is based on the fact that possible losses on short positions are unlimited. On a long position, the maximum loss is 100 percent, even if the price goes to zero, but with a short the theoretical loss could be 1,000 percent if the stock goes from 10, say, to 110. In practice, however, the short seller can control his loss by covering at any point in the rise where he chooses to get out and limit his loss.

Twenty years ago it was believed that if the total short interest on the Big Board exceeded an average day's sales, it would touch off a "short covering rally" in which the short sellers would be massacred. Over the years since then, the short interest, expressed in terms of average daily sales, has increased to the point where it is nearing, and has even on occasion exceeded, twice the daily average, which itself has increased beyond Wall Street's most sanguine projections. Except for the psychological effect it might exert on some traders, there is no fundamental reason why a much higher short interest should interfere with the smooth functioning of the market. In any case, half or more of the total short interest today is due to the activities of arbitragers and specialists, who have less reason to be nervous than do speculators.

THE PROFIT POTENTIAL

The main objective of the discussion up to this point has been to assure the ordinary reader—the individual investor —that there is nothing really wrong, morally or otherwise, with selling short. It should be instructive and encouraging to the relatively inexperienced investor to realize that even the pros have emotional hang-ups when it comes to selling short, and that they even have a tendency to slaughter each other during short covering, with an assist from their computers and the Lemming Syndrome.

There is, however, a great and apparently little-used profit potential on the short side of the market. It *must* be used to enjoy the full benefits of hedging techniques. A glance at any of the performance tables we have studied will confirm this. A fund manager who says that he hopes only to break even on his short positions is in reality confessing that he is not making efficient use of that portion of his funds, and is therefore not taking full advantage of the critical leverage potential. To illustrate, a hedge fund with 30 percent leverage and 70 percent "risk" which is only breaking even on its shorts would perform no better than the unleveraged cash fund of Table 1.

The reasons why some hedge fund managers have failed to take advantage of the profit potential of short selling will be discussed in Section Five.

THE MECHANICS OF SHORT SELLING

The mechanics of short selling are simple enough as far as the investor is concerned, even for the uninitiated. If the stock is trading at about the level at which he wishes to take a short position, the seller simply tells his broker: Short 100 Tulipmanix Corp., or whatever the stock may be called, at the market. The broker does the necessary paper work, and the stock is sold on the next uptick or zero-plus tick.

It is of little concern to the short seller, but the broker, in order to make delivery to the buyer, must borrow the 100 shares somewhere, either within his firm or from an outside lender. The money value of the stock is sent by the broker to the lender and held as collateral until the short sale is covered and the stock is replaced.

Short sales are subject to the same margin requirements as long purchases. Under present (1969) rules the short seller deposits in cash or other collateral 80 percent of the amount of the short sale. No margin is required if the short seller also holds securities convertible into the stock, but this situation should not arise in a hedge fund, as it is not consistent with the efficient use of capital.

No interest is charged on short positions taken on margin, because the proceeds from the sale are enough to supply the collateral required by the lender of the stock. (In fact, when the borrowed stock comes from another account with the same firm, the broker enjoys interest-free use of the proceeds, which he can lend back to his own margin customers at 9 or 10 percent interest.)

If dividends or any other benefits are payable on the stock during the time the short position is held, the short seller must reimburse the lender of the stock. This should be no deterrent to the short seller; a stock selling ex-dividend is, at least theoretically, worth less than before by the amount of the dividend, and this fact is frequently reflected by an adjustment in the market price.

When little demand exists for the loaned stock, the lender may pay interest on the collateral he holds. Ordinarily, however, no interest is paid, and when there is great demand for the stock, the lender may even demand a premium. Stocks for which a premium is required should be avoided by the short seller; if the supply is that tight, it indicates the danger of a "squeeze" at the time of covering.

Every month, usually three business days following the 15th, the total short interest of every NYSE listed stock having a short position of 20,000 shares or more is reported (10,000 for the ASE). These figures, along with the previous month's, are published in the *Wall Street Journal* and other periodicals. The number of listed shares for each NYSE stock is given also. As the short position gets greater in relation to the number of shares outstanding, the risk of a short-covering squeeze increases. It is not generally considered advisable to short stocks having a short interest greater than one half of one percent of the shares outstanding. The trend of the short interest can be estimated by comparing month-to-month figures. Those stocks "possibly involved in arbitrage" are also noted, and this fact of course reduces somewhat the importance of the short total, because the arbitragers will not add materially to a short-covering squeeze.

SOURCES OF INFORMATION AND ASSISTANCE

In sharp contrast to trading long, where a plethora of services of one kind or another is available to the investor, short selling suffers from neglect. Although lists rating stocks "Buy," "Hold" or "Sell" are published, most brokerage houses refuse to name short sale candidates for their run-of-the-mill customers. It is also the policy of many brokerage firms to prohibit their own ordinary salesmen from engaging in short selling for their personal accounts.

So we see that the general prejudice against "the dark side of the market" has not been avoided even by the acknowledged experts in the business. It is not too difficult to find reasons why. Brokers, like most of their customers, share the feeling that short selling is not nice. Also, they are salesmen, and the goods they sell must be made to appear attractive. Why advertise tarnished goods? Moreover, most brokerage houses engage in the very lucrative business of underwriting new issues of both new and established companies, as well as selling secondary issues. Building a clientele in this field would hardly be enhanced by issuing detailed reports on faltering companies—the very ones which may be most needful of fresh injections of capital.

Very little has been published on the subject of selling stocks short. There are a few services whose advertising indicates they can reveal when downturns are due for the market in general, or for particular stocks. Those books and services which the author has examined are based for the most part on so-called technical analysis, or even more esoteric approaches, which are about as successful in predicting downside moves as they are with upswings.

ADVICE FROM HEDGE FUND MANAGERS

Even the hedge fund managers, who should be the real experts in the field of short selling, offer a wide variety of approaches, from analysis of fundamentals to charting and acting on information from Wall Street insiders (a subject that will be examined at the end of this section).

"It's no good selling the high-fliers short," one manager, with the Hubshman Fund, told *Dun's Review*.[4] "In a fast-rising market they can kill you." But another manager, a disciple of the Old Master, said, "We are perfectly willing to short high-fliers . . . if circumstances are right," as in the case of "extremely volatile issues that have overshot the mark and seem destined to come down." However, "If you are convinced the market as a whole is headed lower, then you short blue chips . . . which have plenty of shares outstanding and an active market." Still another hedger reported, "We concentrate on situations where the outlook is really bad; basically, we are looking for companies that could conceivably go out of business."

THE HIGH-FLIERS AS SHORTS

Stocks that qualify as "high-fliers" are those with high volatility, high turnover—particularly on the more volatile trading days, generally high price-earnings ratios, and, quite often, high short interest positions relative to the number of shares outstanding.

A recent and by no means extreme example is Savin Business Machines Corp., ticker symbol SVB on the American Stock Exchange; its main business is electrostatic copying machines; it had never paid a dividend; reported earnings jumped from 27¢ a share in 1967 to 73¢ in 1968. The stock had a big runup in 1968, when the low was $7\frac{1}{2}$, the high 35 (prices adjusted for splits, etc.). In the six previous years the stock had traded generally around 4 or 5, topping at 13 in 1966, and 9 in 1967 (figures rounded). During the first part of 1969 the stock was trading around 30, hitting 32 in anticipation of a stock split, and dropping below 28 soon after the split became effective. In the last part of March the stock took off from 32 on increased volume, rising 1 to 3 points a day for five days, "gapping" on three of those days, and ending at $42\frac{1}{2}$, a new closing high. The price had increased 32 percent in five days, and might have looked like a good short sale to some traders. The price dropped about 4 during the next day, but recovered about half of that by the close. Traders might have concluded, however, that the net loss of 2 confirmed the end of the blow-off stage, and some might have sold short at that point.

In the six days following, the stock rose from $40\frac{1}{2}$ to 52 on increased volume, then dropped 3 on very high volume the next day. Short now? Another drop of 3 the next day; the short looks good. But the next day the price went up 1, and also the next. Cover here? In the next five days the stock dropped 5, then shot up 14 in seven days, but closed on the day's low. Short now?

In the next three months the stock dropped to 47, rebounded to 54, dropped to 40, surged to 54 again, dropped to 35, and bounced up again, each move experiencing, of course, thought-provoking intermediate bobbles.

The market action of SVB has been related in some detail in order to demonstrate the type of stock to avoid in short selling. Even if you have a computer, even with 20/20 hindsight, you can't take the SVB chart and give logical, *consistent* reasons for selecting profitable shorting and covering levels.

Moral: Lay off the volatile high-fliers while they're flying, even if you *know* they're overvalued on a fundamental basis.

Other no-nos: Avoid any stocks with a high short interest; otherwise you may be shot down in the cross fire between the computerized gunslingers. Avoid companies with a small number of shares, especially if they are closely held; covering the short could be costly. Avoid stocks with very low trading volume; a fairly active market is desirable for short covering. Avoid, if you can, potential take-over candidates, which are likely to be weak sisters, and therefore good apparent shorts (but they're fine after the take-over attempt is doomed). Avoid a high short position in a bull market; why buck the trend? (Attuning the short position to the market is considered later under "Hedging: Adjusting the Long/Short Ratio.)

THE GLIDERS AS SHORTS

The quality that is desired in a short sale candidate is the ability to subside gracefully, without sudden flare-ups to annoy and confuse the short seller. Volatility should be fairly low for two months or so before the short sale. However, a volatile past history, followed by a cooling of investor interest, is quite acceptable. After all, there had to be some reason in the past for the stock to rise above its true value. Recent daily volume should be moderate. Occasional high-volume days, especially down days perhaps representing institutional unloading, are quite acceptable.

The stock should already be headed down, and there should be nothing in the fundamentals to indicate any reason for a reversal in the trend.

If there is a good number of shares outstanding, if the stock is selling at a relatively high price-earnings ratio, and if the overall market is headed down, the situation is really ripe for selling short.

Even a cursory examination of the charts published by such companies as Treadline and Geiergraph for 1968 and 1969 shows that literally scores of stocks exhibited most or all of the desired characteristics going into the bear market of 1969.

For example, Bangor Punta went from a January high of around 50 to a mid-year low of 25 (and didn't stop there). The largest recovery movement during the entire period was just under 3 points (closing quotations), which should not have disturbed the sleep of the most insomniac hedge fund manager.

Castleton Industries dropped from over 16 in January to under 8 at mid-year, and never came back as much as 2 points during that time.

Commercial Solvents dropped from 30 to 17 in the same period, with a maximum recovery of 3.

The three examples above were cited first only because they happened to be near the head of the alphabet. Many others displayed the same characteristics. Diversified Industries dropped from 50 to 23, with a maximum recovery of 4. Other examples: General Dynamics, 48 to 29 (3); Gulf & Western, 52 to 25 (5); Lockheed, 49 to 27 (3); and so on, including McDonnell Douglas, Pan American World Airways, Ronson, and World Airways, all with big drops and bobbles of 3 or less.

In many cases, the stocks did not wait for the bear market to begin their own drops, but had been in a general decline for a year of two. This indicates, contrary to the conventional wisdom, that it is *not* necessary to catch a stock near its high in order to make a good short sale.

Pan American Sulphur Co. is fairly representative of this group. Pasco, with 4.8 million shares out, enjoyed almost a glamour status at one time, after it succeeded in breaking into the sulphur oligopoly dominated by Texas Gulf and Freeport. With increasing sales and earnings, the stock rose from under 8 (adjusted) in 1962 to 28 in March 1966. It backed and filled for two years, then rose to an all-time high of just over 46 in November 1967, about the time Susquehanna Corp. began its take-over attempt (an issue still unresolved two years later).

Pasco's troubles had begun even earlier, with harassment from the Mexican government through export controls— harassment that culminated in *de facto* expropriation when the company was pressured into selling 66 percent of its

Mexican subsidiary, which owned all of Pasco's sulphur reserves and production facilities. However, the forced sale put Pasco in a nice cash position, of which Susquehanna was not unmindful. As the struggle for control continued through 1968, the stock fluctuated between 41 and 27. During the year the average price-earnings ratio was 29, an all-time high for the stock, and fairly rich for any chemical company, but especially so for one which had lost 66 percent of its sulphur reserves and production, practically its only source of income.

Adding to Pasco's troubles was a weakening in sulphur prices due to accelerating production and mineral discoveries by competing companies. Earnings dropped and the dividend was cut to the point where Susquehanna, which now owned over 40 percent of Pasco's stock, must have been wondering how it was going to service the debt it had contracted to buy the Pasco shares. To make matters worse, Susquehanna had a huge paper loss on its investment, and any attempt to raise money by selling Pasco stock would change the loss from paper to concrete.

This is where the situation stood at the onset of the 1969 bear market: a worsening sulphur market, prospects for further declines in earnings and dividends, the take-over attempt still up in the air, a big block of stock, so to speak, overhanging the market, and no good news in sight.

All of these facts had been published and were available to the potential short seller as 1969 began. Pan American Sulphur stock glided gracefully from its January high of 35½ to 17 at mid-year (and kept going down from there). The maximum recovery moves were two one-day efforts of less than 3 points each, neither move on much volume.

Susquehanna, incidentally, was an even better short sale candidate. Its common got as high as 80 in 1968, but it was still near 39 as 1969 began. By mid-year it had fallen to 13, a further drop of 67 percent, and it did not stop there. The maximum recovery move in this case was just over 2 points, on high volume.

In sum, the gliders, or the shot-down high-fliers, are much preferable to the active high-fliers as short sale candidates.

This is because there is some fundamental logic behind, some factual basis for, the behavior of the gliders, while there is literally no way to predict to what peaks emotional (and perhaps computerized) trading will push a popular stock, nor what the extent of the wild gyrations will be for either the ascent or the descent which will follow. Fund managers and ordinary traders who complain of getting "whiplashed" are trying to divine the gyrations of the high-fliers.

We have said that there is some known basis for the behavior of the gliders, and therefore for selling them short. To some extent, at least, this may seem to contradict another hoary Wall Street maxim: Don't sell on the bad news. Not the instant it crosses the tape, perhaps, but the informed trader must respond to factual and fundamental bad news, particularly when no good news is in sight. If the bad news, for example, is that the company's properties are facing expropriation; that there is overproduction in the industry; that there is price-cutting; that earnings are lower and the dividend may be cut; and if the bad news is cumulative, it is wise to cut and run—or sell short.

Certainly one type of bad news is a sell signal in these days of hyperemphasis on growth: official admission that a company's earnings will fall short of those which had been projected earlier, or will actually drop.

SUMMARY

This chapter was written to assure the incipient hedger that profitable short selling is not only morally right and economically useful, but absolutely essential to the optimum application of hedge fund techniques in the management of capital. A complete course in short selling could not be charted in a single chapter, but some useful guideposts have perhaps been erected for those about to explore this interesting and potentially rewarding field.

Methods for measuring the risk in short sales and for setting the long/short ratio are described next.

Hedging: adjusting the long/short ratio

IS HEDGING REALLY BEING USED?

THE MOST striking fact about hedging is that hedge fund managers, according to all reports, have put it to so little use in achieving their announced objective of maximum capital appreciation.

As we demonstrated in Section Two, the mere fact that a fund is hedged does not add one cent to its performance potential, but judicious *adjustment* of the longs and shorts to keep in tune with market trends, as we saw earlier in this section, could nearly double performance. Table 3 also indicated the profit potential of higher short positions in bear markets.

However, hedge fund managers, as we have already noted, seem content to break even on their shorts, and even the Old Master admits to shortcomings in judging market trends. "Our market judgment," *Business Week*[2] quotes Jones, "really hasn't been good in the last few years, but our stock selections have made up for it." *Fortune*[1] said that Jones had a high "risk" position of 140 percent in the early part of 1962. "As the market declined, he gradually increased his short position, but not as quickly as he should have. His losses that spring were heavy, and his investors ended up with a small

75

loss for the fiscal year," his only losing year. "After the break, furthermore, he turned bearish and so did not at first benefit from the market's recovery."

Donald F. Woodward, described as Jones' right-hand man, told *Dun's Review*,[4] "Over the years . . . our judgment about the prevailing market trend has not been our strong point. It makes my mouth water to think how well we might have done if it had been."

The last sentence certainly indicates an awareness of the potential noted earlier. To conclude, then, as the *Fortune* writer apparently did, that the *main advantage* of the hedge concept "is that the investor's short position enables him to operate on the long side with maximum aggressiveness," is simply to overlook the main advantages. The real advantages, it may be, are not being taken advantage of—but they are there.

"Typically," noted *Business Week*, "Jones is only modestly net long." This means, of course, that his short position is generally substantial, so if he does little better than break even on his shorts, his longs must do all the work. *Fortune* tends to confirm this: Jones' individual stock selections "have generally been brilliant." We can't help wondering how much better he might have done without the drag of having so much of his capital tied up in unprofitable shorts; that is, if he had simply concentrated on his brilliant longs.

According to *Business Week*, "Jones concedes that at times his 'risk factor' has drifted upward in a bull market without any conscious effort."

"Our managers had the same complacent pull on them as the whole Street," the article quoted him, but Jones does believe that performance can be improved if "risk" can be measured better, and he also hopes to improve his "velocity ratings."

This brings us back to the basics of the hedge funders—the concepts of "risk" and velocity. These were defined in the first section and referred to throughout the text. Now let's look more closely at their validity and usefulness.

"RISK" IS NOT RISK

First, "risk," as defined by the hedge funders, is not synonymous with *risk*, as defined by the dictionaries, or as generally understood in the field of investments.

The dictionary definition of *risk* is *exposure to the chance of loss or injury.*

The hedgers' "risk" is exposure, true: the difference between the longs and the shorts, expressed as a percentage of unleveraged capital. But remember, the hedge fund is not a true hedge. The longs can go down; the shorts can go up. Every dollar invested, long or short, paid-in or borrowed, is exposed to real risk.

Therefore, the higher the leverage, the greater the risk. By the hedgers' definition, however, a cash hedge investing 85 long and 15 short has a "risk" of 70 percent, *exactly the same* as that of the hedge fund which doubles its capital by borrowing and invests 135 long and 65 short. Obviously, the real risk in the latter case is double that in the former.

Moreover, a "risk" of zero is obtained by investing half long and half short. Does this mean that risk has been eliminated? Obviously not. All funds are still exposed to risk. And of course, "negative risk" doesn't mean what it says either.

All in all, we find the term "risk" somewhat confusing if not actually misleading. It is certainly not the same thing as *risk,* which is an important element in fund management of all kinds—and one that should be kept free of confusion. "Risk" *is* a way of expressing the proportion of longs to shorts, but this can be more easily and usefully expressed, as we shall see presently, by the long/short ratio.

The reader, of course, is free to use either, or both. This book gives examples of each.

HEDGING AND RISK

While hedging does not eliminate risk, it can still serve some very useful purposes, as we mentioned earlier.

Hedging can *moderate* the effect of sudden or unexpected market swings on the total worth of the portfolio, thereby giving the fund manager the time and the opportunity to adjust the "risk," or the proportion of longs and shorts, to take account of changing conditions. In this sense, hedging can help to reduce risk—even though an *increase* in "risk" might well be involved.

Also, hedging allows the fund manager to take advantage of good shorts as well as good longs. In a bear market, in which the declining stocks outnumber those rising, the simple probability of selecting a successful short over a successful long is evident. In this sense, too, risk is in effect reduced by hedging.

In addition, hedging permits full investment of funds during a bear market (in contrast to the usual strategy, used by mutual funds and others, of increasing the cash position). In this sense, hedging *increases* the risk.

MEASURES OF RISK

Graham and Dodd, in their book *Security Analysis,* the fundamentalists' bible, never bother to define risk, although they are much concerned with avoiding it (somewhat as one would avoid sin without thinking it necessary to define it).

In the financial sense, risk is uncertainty as it relates to capital investments, and applies to receipt of income as well as return of principal. With hedge funds, the overriding concern is what may happen to the principal. This kind of uncertainty, or exposure to loss, is now generally expressed by the term *volatility,* a measure of stock price deviation from some standard.

In this sense, the term has not yet appeared in Graham and Dodd, or even the unabridged dictionary. We can only wonder why the familiar term *variation* has been avoided by everyone except theoreticians; besides being more descriptive, it has the advantage that statistical science has several useful measures for quantifying it. In any case, volatility and variability share the synonym *fickleness,* which is a good one for us to keep in mind.

The hedge funders have sidestepped both volatility and variation, in favor of the term *velocity*. It means about the same thing: "Speed Kills." Velocity, as noted in Section One, is a rating assigned to a stock according to its chart activity over a certain period compared to some selected standard, such as Standard & Poor's 500-stock index. One analyst and hedge fund manager[3] suggests a five-year comparison with the Standard & Poor's 500 as the standard. Jones is said to use a six-month period and the same index. By some method not revealed in the *Fortune* article, Jones came up with velocity ratings of 6.61 for Syntex and 1.72 for Kerr-McGee. These are examples of the multipliers used to arrive at adjusted dollars and adjusted "risk."

According to *Business Week,* "Jones is still not satisfied with his velocity ratings and constantly is trying to refine them."

Indeed, some questions do arise. For instance, how useful is historical volatility? Some of the hottest high-fliers take off from a chart pattern as calm as the Sea of Tranquility. Natomas hardly got above 10 for years, then really took off like a rocket, and many other stocks have followed a similar pattern. The farther back any volatility measure goes, the less relevant it is. No doubt a very precise figure can be calculated by using a five-year, or even longer, base, but how useful is it? Six months is a more reasonable base period; the real need, however, is for a figure which can be projected into the future with some confidence, and for most hedge funders that means the near future.

Whatever may be the base period or the method of calculation, how useful is a velocity rating like 6.61? True, it can be used to multiply an exact figure in dollars, but the end result of the calculations is only "risk." Unless a method is employed to select the *right* "risk" with the same degree of accuracy, it would seem permissible to drop a digit or two from such velocity figures.

Complications arise also in keeping the calculations current. The velocity rating is a moving average, and therefore requires constant updating. Even the stock prices used in calculating "risk" should reflect current prices, not the original investment. It all adds up to a lot of work, especially for those without a computer.

Small wonder then that most hedge fund operators (although many perform some version of "risk" and velocity calculations) pay only lip service to the "risk" concept. As *Business Week* noted, "Some consider it only a 'post facto expression' of market judgment."

But the hedge concept *is* valid and useful, as we have seen, and management of a hedge fund necessitates some logical method of setting the "risk," which is actually the division of the portfolio between longs and shorts. Moreover, volatility is real also, and should be considered in setting the long/short ratio.

In defining risk as exposure to *loss,* we are overlooking something very important to the investment decision-making process. Risk is a two-sided coin; the other side is exposure to *gain.* A stodgy stock with low volatility may not present much risk of loss, but it probably won't gain much either. Volatility is therefore not merely a measure of risk, but also of opportunity. Furthermore, neither risk nor opportunity are measured accurately or completely by any velocity or volatility factor, even if it could remain constant for a particular stock.

Equally important is *the price at which the stock is purchased.* This factor can vary the risk and opportunity over a wide range, even though the volatility remains unchanged. A fairly simple method for taking this fact into account in determining risk will be suggested presently.

The degree of risk assumed by any fund should depend upon its particular goals, and the amount of overall risk it is willing to assume to achieve those goals. Risk and potential gain are trade-offs, *provided* that the stocks with the desired risk are the best in their category, and the price is right. In other words, just because a stock is risky does not mean it has a high profit potential. Risk can also be controlled to some extent by diversification. Generally speaking, the lower the number of stocks, the higher the risk, and the higher the profit potential.

We must conclude, then, that velocity, although it is *a*

measure of risk, is not comprehensive enough to be used as the sole multiplier in arriving at adjusted dollars.

Those hedge funders who, like the majority, wish to avoid the troublesome business of applying velocity and other measures of risk can still reflect the concept by their selection of longs and shorts for the portfolio. A stock's volatility can be estimated quickly by glancing at its recent chart action; no precise figures are needed, for the eyeball can quickly separate stocks into "High," "Medium" and "Low" risk. These judgments can be modified, if necessary, by the current price level of the stock; the overall risk is increased or decreased depending upon whether the stock is selling near its high or its low.

Having judged the risk in this manner, in strong upward market movements, the high-risk stocks among the longs can be increased. In bear markets, the high-risk shorts can be increased, while lower risk stocks among the longs are emphasized. In sideways or chicken markets, high-risk stocks among both longs and shorts can be reduced and maintained more or less in balance.

THE RISKOP FACTOR: A MEASURE OF BOTH RISK AND OPPORTUNITY

For those readers who want a quantitative measure that takes account of opportunity as well as risk, and one which can be used as a multiplier for adjusting both the long and short positions, we offer the Risk-Opportunity Factor, or the *Riskop Factor*, for short.

The Riskop Factor for any stock can be calculated in seconds, using the year's high and low and the current price figures from the daily newspaper:

$$\text{Riskop Factor (for longs)} = \frac{\text{High} - \text{Low}}{\text{Average Price}} + \frac{\text{Price} - \text{Average Price}}{\text{Average Price}}$$

Substituting letters for words:

$$R_l = \frac{H - L}{\frac{1}{2}(H + L)} + \frac{P - \frac{1}{2}(H + L)}{\frac{1}{2}(H + L)}$$

Let's consider the two component terms in order. $H - L$, the difference between the high and the low, is the *range*, a well-known measure of variation, and the simplest. Dividing the range, $H - L$, by $\frac{1}{2}(H + L)$ relates the variation to the average price as a base or standard; the lower the average price, the more significant the size of the variation, and vice versa.

The term

$$\frac{H - L}{\frac{1}{2}(H + L)}$$

is therefore a measure of volatility, which in turn is a measure of risk.

The second term,

$$\frac{P - \frac{1}{2}(H + L)}{\frac{1}{2}(H + L)},$$

is simply the difference between the current price and the average price, related to the average price. If we assume that the average price is the normal one to which the present price will tend to return, the difference between the two is a measure of either risk or opportunity, depending upon whether the current price is above or below the average price.

For example, Syntex, currently at 77, has had a yearly high to date of 87 and a low of 49. Its Riskop Factor is therefore:

$$R_l = \frac{87 - 49}{68} + \frac{77 - 68}{68} = \frac{38}{68} + \frac{9}{68} = .56 + .13 = .69$$

The amount .56 is the measure of risk due to the range or volatility. The amount .13 is added to this because the stock is now selling above its average price, toward which it will probably return sooner or later—a condition which increases the risk due to volatility alone.

Kerr-McGee (high 125, low 81, price 101) is an example of a stock selling below its average price; the opportunity term is therefore subtractive, because the risk is reduced.

$$R_l = \frac{125 - 81}{103} + \frac{101 - 103}{103} = \frac{44}{103} + \frac{-2}{103} = .43 - .02 = .41$$

The above values for R_l would be used to adjust the dollar amounts of the stocks already in, or being considered for, the long side of the portfolio.

However, when considering shorts, although the first, or volatility, term remains the same, the concepts of risk and opportunity are reversed in the second term. In other words, a stock sold short above its average price will probably go down (opportunity), while one sold short below its average price will probably go up (risk). The Riskop Factor for shorts therefore has a minus sign instead of a plus sign between the two terms of the formula:

$$R_s = \frac{H - L}{\frac{1}{2}(H + L)} - \frac{P - \frac{1}{2}(H + L)}{\frac{1}{2}(H + L)}$$

If Syntex, then, is being considered for a short instead of a long, its Riskop Factor is:

$$R_s = .56 - .13 = .43$$

As a long, Syntex has a Riskop Factor of .69. If a stock is selling closer to its high than to its low, doesn't it seem logical that it would make a riskier long than a short?

For Kerr-McGee as a short:

$$R_s = .43 + .02 = .45$$

Although there is little difference between the long and short risks for Kerr-McGee, which is selling near its average price, there is a substantial difference for Syntex, because it is currently selling well above its average price.

This difference would not be shown by the conventional measures of volatility, which give the same values for longs and shorts. The Riskop Factor is therefore a useful measure, over and above its possible use to calculate adjusted dollars.

Let's return now to the two terms of the Riskop formulas. We have said that the term

$$\frac{H - L}{\frac{1}{2}(H + L)}$$

is a measure of volatility. It is obviously at a minimum, zero, when there is no price change at all, that is, when $H = L$, which would be the case, for example, with cash. A very stable security, such as a high grade bond during times of steady interest rates, would have a volatility near zero.

The maximum theoretical value of

$$\frac{H-L}{\frac{1}{2}(H+L)}$$

is equal to 2, when $L=0$. All intermediate values between zero and 2 are theoretically possible, but the great majority of stocks will fall somewhere between .1 and 1.3.

The term

$$\frac{P-\frac{1}{2}(H+L)}{\frac{1}{2}(H+L)}$$

can be, as we have seen, a measure either of additional risk or of opportunity. Its value is zero when the current price is the same as the average price. The maximum possible value for this term is $+1$, when the present price equals the high, and the low is zero. The minimum theoretical value is -1, when both the low and the current price are equal to zero.

We now have as limits for the two terms:

for $\dfrac{H-L}{\frac{1}{2}(H+L)}$, minimum 0; maximum $+2$

for $\dfrac{P-\frac{1}{2}(H+L)}{\frac{1}{2}(H+L)}$, minimum -1; maximum $+1$

When values of R_l are calculated, these limits apply to their respective terms. However, the mathematical conditions that result in a minus value for the second term always result in an equal or greater positive value for the first term. In other words, the value of R_l cannot drop below zero, because the second term, when it is subtracted, can never exceed the first. Therefore the total possible range for R_l is from zero (lowest risk) to 3 (very high risk).

The limits for R_s, the Riskop Factor for shorts, can be determined in similar fashion. As before, the limits for the first term are zero and $+2$.

The term

$$-\frac{P - \frac{1}{2}(H+L)}{\frac{1}{2}(H+L)}$$

can vary between $+1$, when the current price and the low are both equal to zero, and -1, when the current price equals the high and the low is zero. Because the first term in the formula

$$R_s = \frac{H-L}{\frac{1}{2}(H+L)} - \frac{P - \frac{1}{2}(H+L)}{\frac{1}{2}(H+L)}$$

is always equal to or greater than the second, R_s can never be less than zero. The limits for R_s are therefore zero (for lowest possible risk) and 3 (for highest possible risk), the same as the limits for R_l.

In calculating actual values for R_l and R_s using the formulas, it is not necessary to remember these limits for the individual terms or for the Riskop Factors themselves; the formulas take care of the limits and the plus and minus signs.

We have noted that although both formulas take into account the element of opportunity (represented by a minus value), the *net* values for R_l and R_s are always *positive*. In other words, there is always *some* risk in both long and short positions in stocks. A net negative value would indicate a sure thing, which is hard to come by, even for a hedge funder.

Now let's calculate a few more values for Riskop Factors before applying them to a theoretical hedge fund portfolio.

Pan American Sulphur (high 36, low 15, price 16)

$$R_l = \frac{36-15}{25.5} + \frac{16-25.5}{25.5} = \frac{21}{25.5} + \frac{-9.5}{25.5} = .82 - .37 = .45$$

$$R_s = .82 + .37 = 1.19$$

These values for R contrast Pasco's high risk as a short (1.19) at current prices with its relatively low risk as a long (0.45).

Milgo Electronics (high 61, low 18, price 55)

$$R_l = \frac{61-18}{39.5} + \frac{55-39.5}{39.5} = \frac{43}{39.5} + \frac{15.5}{39.5} = 1.09 + .39 = 1.48$$

$$R_s = 1.09 - .39 = .70$$

Here the calculations indicate that at current price levels
Milgo is over twice as risky as a long as it is as a short. We'll
short it in our portfolio.

Xerox (high 115, low 85, price 105)

$$R_l = \frac{115 - 85}{100} + \frac{105 - 100}{100} = \frac{30}{100} + \frac{5}{100} = .30 + .05 = .35$$

$$R_s = .30 - .05 = .25$$

The results show that at current price levels the former
high-flier is not very risky either as a long or a short. Although
Xerox is somewhat riskier as a long, we shall use it as such
in our portfolio.

A PORTFOLIO USING ADJUSTED DOLLARS

The values for Riskop Factors calculated above can be applied to an imaginary portfolio in order to illustrate the simple
calculations involved in arriving at adjusted dollars and
"risk."

TABLE 4

Calculation of adjusted dollars

Stock	Shares	Price	Dollars	R	Adjusted Dollars Longs	Shorts
Xerox (long)	200	105	21,000	.35	7,400	
Pan A Sul (long) ...	1000	16	16,000	.45	7,200	
Kerr-Mc (short)	100	101	10,100	.45		4,500
Milgo (short)	100	55	5,500	.70		3,900
			52,600		14,600	8,400

The total dollars invested in both longs and shorts add up
to $52,600. Assume that the fund or individual has added to
$35,000 paid-in capital by borrowing or otherwise leveraging
about 50 percent more, or $17,600.

Using *un*adjusted dollars,

$$\text{"Risk"} = \frac{37,000 - 15,600}{35,000} = 61\%$$

In using adjusted dollars to calculate "risk," the $35,000 of paid-in capital must be reduced in the same proportion that dollars have been reduced to adjusted dollars.

$$\text{Adjusted paid-in capital} = \frac{23,000}{52,600} \times 35,000 = 15,300$$

$$\text{Adjusted "risk"} = \frac{14,600 - 8,400}{15,300} = 40.5\%$$

The determinations of "risk"—unadjusted and adjusted—differ by wide margins in this example.

At least as useful as the adjusted "risk" and even easier to calculate is the long-short ratio using adjusted dollars:

$$\text{Adjusted L/S ratio} = \frac{14,600}{8,400} = \frac{64}{36}$$

This ratio shows that 64 percent of the adjusted dollars are invested long, with 36 percent in short positions. These are the figures we need to know in order to make use of the method for adjusting the long/short ratio to keep in tune with the prevailing market described in the following pages.

First, however, a few words of advice on the use of the Riskop Factor calculations. The figures are probably significant to no more than one place after the decimal point; they have been carried out farther here for illustrative purposes.

Also, it should be remembered that the high and low figures published in the newspapers cover an increasing time span, generally starting with three months on or about March 31, and building up to a year and three months before a new start is made. Because longs and shorts are affected similarly, this does not seem to present any great difficulty. Purists can, if they wish to take the trouble, maintain their own high and low figures for a constant period of three months, or whatever.

More finely tuned values for R could no doubt be obtained by replacing range, $H - L$ in the formula, with a more sensitive measure of variation—the standard deviation, for example. In addition, the average price, $\frac{1}{2}(H + L)$, in the top line of the second term, could well be replaced by a *projected* price, based on the analysis of a particular stock.

However, refinements of this type require much more time, effort, knowledge and experience than the simple method suggested.

In any case, the formula is not to be followed blindly. If, for example, you have good reason to believe that the price of a depressed stock is not going to recover to anywhere near its average price within the time period you're interested in, simply use a more judicious price, based on your assessment of the situation, in place of the average price in the top line of the second term.

Further refinements in the formula would seem to offer opportunities for computer analysis. (We promised to eschew any mention of multiple regression.)

SETTING THE LONG/SHORT RATIO

Nowhere in the literature published to date has any hedge fund manager revealed how he goes about *deciding* just what the "risk" should be at any given time. Even the Old Master admits that his success depends much more upon brilliant selection of stocks than upon his judgment on the general trend of the market, and that he even lost a little ground one year because of misjudgment of the trends.

Every fund manager, and indeed every investor, has the same problem: how to determine what the trend is, how long it will last, how to recognize a reversal when it occurs, and what action to take on specific stocks.

No matter what the direction of the market may be, millions of shares change hands every trading day, and there is a buyer for every seller—which would seem to indicate that at least half the people are confused all the time.

The technicians are applying rules they don't even agree on among themselves to every chart they can lay their hands on, from charts of individual stocks to those of the various averages. As a result of their differing technical interpretations, a lot of stock no doubt changes hands among the technicians themselves. And we must also assume that the fundamentalists, after studying the same fundamentals, are selling stock to each other. How else can block trading among funds and other institutional investors be explained?

To help in the basic matter of judging trends, there are literally scores of indexes available. Most fundamental of all are the economic indicators, and these are fed into computers programmed with various econometric models in order to better divine stock trends.

Even more directly related to the stock market, there are the charts of the various Dow Jones averages, those of Standard & Poor's and the *New York Times;* the various NYSE indexes, the short-range oscillator, the short interest ratio; the Standard & Poor's low-priced stock index; the odd-lot index and odd-lot short sales (these two based on the premise that the little guy is so consistently confused that the smart operator can make wise decisions just by watching him and doing the opposite); also brokers' free credit and net debit balances; and Barron's Confidence Index.

There is even—honest to God!—the *Revelation Index.* This one is among those created or supplied by *Indicator Digest,* whose former editor, you recall, was charged by the SEC with dealing in stocks his service was about to say nice things about. (Current officers were not involved.)

Many of the indexes are not lacking in charm, or even a certain utility. The trouble is, they're not really very reliable guides for decision making in the stock market. Consider the widely heralded Barron's Confidence Index, which, by indicating the relative preference of "smart money" for high-grade and speculative bonds, is believed to give some advance indication of money flow in and out of the stock market. It is one of the most saw-toothed indexes conceived to date; hardly a week goes by without a reversal in trend. In the author's opinion, it is probably a good indicator of the relative preference of both smart and dumb money for high-grade and speculative bonds.

However, the hedge funder should not yield to despair because of contrary and indecisive indexes. He has, in hedging, a unique tool for prospering under such conditions, provided he has some method for keeping attuned to the market.

As we pointed out earlier, the improvements in performance made possible by keeping attuned are quite remarkable. Moreover, the hedge fund manager can take a pragmatic view toward his portfolio adjustments, shifting the proportion of longs and shorts to keep in tune with market conditions as they are revealed to him.

But even if he can decide the course of the market by examination of the various indexes, how can he set the actual amount of money to invest long and the amount to invest short? It would improve his odds in selecting both longs and shorts if he could make some sense out of how many stocks are trending upward and how many are trending downward.

The advance-decline line, supplied by various services, is of some help, but it is a single line, the result of the *difference* between the longs and the shorts, not the actual amounts of each. More useful would be *two* curves, one for advances and another for declines, on the order of the upside-downside *volume* curves which are available.

The hedge funder can, like the author, prepare his own tables and curves, using the daily figures for advances and declines appearing in the *Wall Street Journal* and other newspapers.

To smooth out the day-to-day irregularities, it is necessary to calculate moving averages for both the advances and declines. This is simple enough. To obtain a 10-day moving average for the advances, for example, the number of advances for each of the 10 trading days is totaled and divided by 10. On the following day, the new figure for advances is added to the former total, the oldest one (11 days back) is subtracted, and the new moving average is obtained by dividing by 10. The moving average for the declines is obtained in the same manner.

During the first week of November 1969, for example, the advances on the NYSE ranged from 654 to 836, a difference of 182. The moving average during the same period ranged from 682 to 720, a difference of only 38, indicating the dampening effect of the moving average.

The declines during the week ranged from 533 to 704, a

difference of 171; the moving average ranged from 659 to 679, a difference of only 20.

The percentage of advances at any given time is obtained by dividing the moving average figure for advances by the sum of the advance and decline figures. The decline percentage, of course is then obtained most easily by subtracting the advance percentage from 100. During the week mentioned, the advances varied from 50 to 52 percent, while the declines, of course, varied between 50 and 48 percent.

These percentages can be applied directly to determine what the dollar or adjusted dollar amounts of longs and shorts in the hedge fund portfolio should be at any given time, in order to keep in tune with the market.

The ratio of longs to shorts during the week mentioned could well have been set at approximately 50-50. Earlier in the year, say the first half of March, a 40-60 ratio of longs to shorts would have been more appropriate.

Although the number of figures following the decimal point to which these percentages can be calculated is limited only by your supply of paper, no useful purpose is served by going beyond the nearest percentage point, and in applying the figures to a portfolio even wider margins are feasible.

The 10-day advance-decline moving averages reflect quite closely the NYSE composite index. Therefore, relating your individual portfolio to the moving averages in the manner suggested will indeed keep you in tune with the market. You can be certain, also, that you will not miss important reversals or changes in trends, as even some of the experts have done.

However, the advance/decline averages that we have described reflect all the stocks on the Big Board. Your portfolio consists of a relatively few individual issues. If they are performing well, a fairly wide variation from the indicated L/S ratio is acceptable. But if you have any shorts which are rising and longs which are falling, they should be weeded out and replaced with issues that move the portfolio more in line with the desired L/S ratio.

Interestingly enough, the indicated percentage of longs, when plotted on graph paper, often peaks out or bottoms ahead of the composite index. This could help in timing, but it is not necessary to the success of hedging. The beauty of hedging is that it works even if there is a *lag* in making adjustments, as long as the general L/S proportions are observed.

Stock selection, of course, is still extremely important, but even here the *probability* of making good selections is improved by observing the L/S ratios.

The foregoing has illustrated how separate moving averages of daily advances and declines can be used to determine and adjust the long/short ratios in hedge portfolios. The possible variations and refinements are numerous. The hedger should select a system to fit his individual needs, perferably after some dry runs with theoretical portfolios.

A 10-day moving average was used for illustration, but longer periods of 30, 60, or 90 days will not only smooth out the plotted curves (of the desired long percentage, most practically), but will be even more indicative of longer term trends. Such longer term curves still remain quite responsive to current market changes. A little experimentation by the reader will prove rewarding.

For example, the author has found 4-week moving averages useful when used in conjunction with the 10-day averages. They are obtained in the same manner as the latter, except that the weekly totals for advances and declines are used in the calculations, instead of the daily figures. The resultant curve is much smoother, and therefore a steadier guide for adjusting the long/short ratio, and it still remains generally in tune with the NYSE composite index. During 1969, for example, the indicated percentage of longs stayed below 50 percent most of the time, reaching a low of 33 over a month before the index bottomed out, then trending upward to a high of 56 as the index peaked in early November, and falling to 36 along with the December sell-off. Throughout the year, the more sensitive 10-day moving average generally peaked out well in advance of the NYSE index.

Another possible variation is the use of the advance and decline figures of the American Stock Exchange to calculate the moving averages. The long-percentage curve can be used both in adjusting ASE stocks in the portfolio and in "confirming" the NYSE curve.

The ideal moving averages for our purposes would reflect other factors in addition to the *number* of advances and declines, which indicates only the direction of the price changes. The *amount* of each price change and the *volume* of shares traded are also significant. However, until such ideal averages become generally available, those of us without computers have a quite satisfactory tool available in some adaption of the advance/decline moving averages.

No matter what specific method is used to determine the desirable long and short percentages, remember that the results are only guidelines, not surefire formulas for success. Although such hedging does increase the odds on successful selection and timing, these last factors are still very important.

Remember also that the long/short determinations do not constitute a rigid formula. The odds on successful stock selection are not determined solely by the number of advances and declines, so the hedger should feel free to make some adjustments in order to adapt the method to his particular requirements. If he is convinced, for example, that his ability to select good longs is definitely better than his ability to pick good shorts, he can adjust the indicated long/short ratios to take this into account, by increasing the indicated longs by, say, 10 percent, and decreasing the shorts by the same number of percentage points. In other words, if the indicated L/S ratio is 60-40, the adjusted ratio would be 70-30.

However, if such an adjustment is made, it should be done on a consistent basis, so that changes in market trends will be noted and acted upon.

Maneuverability and turnover

ONE of the reasons given for the success of the hedge funds is their maneuverability. They are usually organized in such a way that the portfolio managers can act immediately on decisions to buy or sell, with no need for committee consultation and approval.

Size can detract somewhat from maneuverability (although fund managers show a tendency to revise upward their ideas on maneuverable limits as their own funds increase in size). Large holdings of some stocks may be difficult to unload in a falling market, and sizeable short sales may be even harder to accomplish. Some large hedge funds, both public and private, minimize this impediment to maneuverability by dividing the capital among a number of autonomous fund managers, who then have the added incentive of internal competition.

Another advantage attributed to the hedge funds is that their short positions allow them to take a more "aggressive" stance, which results in higher turnover. Losses on shorts, because they are always short term for tax purposes, can be used to offset short-term gains on the longs. Gains on the shorts themselves can be taken at any time, for there is no tax reason to hold the positions any longer than necessary.

Maneuverability and turnover are stepped up by gun-slinger-type fund managers who engage in computer free-for-alls and other go-go operations. Cutting losses can also increase turnover. According to the *Los Angeles Times*,[17] a prominent (but unnamed) securities executive claimed that "9 out of 10 transactions by hedge funds are losing ones; the hedgers play for the big one, cutting their losing ones loose quickly."

Hedge fund managers seem to have just as much trouble making short-term killings as the ordinary investor. "We don't make a great deal" of money by trading, one manager told *Barron's*.[25] "Maybe some people are better at it than we are, or maybe some people just talk a better game."

Probably a majority of the hedge funds limit trading in their winning long stocks as a matter of policy in order to make sure that the gains will be long term for tax purposes. Those private hedge fund partnerships whose investors may be in a 70 or 77 percent bracket for short-term gains have a real incentive to wait six months for the long-term tax treatment, where Uncle takes no more than 25 percent.

Of course, the individual investor who does not share the mixed blessings of high income can feel less constrained about trading, including short selling, which results in short-term gains.

Aside from the baneful effect of taxes, trading can have a charm of its own. Probably as much harm has been done by holding a stock too long as by selling too soon.

We buy a stock, say, at 20. It does nothing much for three weeks or so, then goes up to 23 in a few days. We note happily that it is headed in the right direction. Two months later it is down to 17. Perhaps it stays there or drops lower, and we sell before the six-month holding period to take a short-term loss.

Or perhaps we are lucky; the price climbs slowly but steadily for the rest of the year, and we sell at 25⅝ for a profit of 5, even after the broker has got his going both ways. We make 25 percent on our investment. Not too bad; better than a lot of mutual funds. The gain is long term, too.

But suppose we had got out at 22⅝ after the first month. That's a gain of 2, after the broker takes his, or 10 percent a month. Even without compounding, that's 120 percent a year. Compounded—which is what it would be if we could do as well with our money every month—the annual gain would be 214 percent, or $42.80 on the original $20. If we're in a 50 percent tax bracket, we clear $21.40—compared to $3.75 after a 25 percent tax on a long-term gain of $5 in the first example.

For the hedger, the type of turnover described above is consistent with the efficient use of capital, and the magic of compounding is always available. Let's say we start with $10,000 capital, which we increase to $15,000 by leveraging. With annual compounding of 40 percent capital gains after taxes, our stake will grow to $1 million in $12\frac{1}{2}$ years.

In Section One it was noted that if the original investors who put $100,000 into Jones' hedge fund in 1949 had left all of their profits in, the total by 1966 would have grown to nearly $5 million. That represents a compounded annual growth rate of 26 percent, *before* taxes, apparently. How they would have paid their taxes if they had left all of their profits in is a matter for conjecture, but being rich in the first place would have helped.

Brokerage fees and
inside sources of information

BROKERAGE FEES, which are especially burdensome with high turnover, are considered by most normal investors to be almost as odious as taxes. Many of the hedge funds, however, have been able to put this necessary evil to work for them.

Fortune reported that, due to his high turnover, "the weight Jones swings on Wall Street is many times magnified by the fact that, like all hedge-fund operators, he is a prodigious producer of commissions." One brokerage house executes practically all of Jones' orders, but keeps only about half of the commissions for itself. The other half, in the form of "give-up" checks, is turned over to certain other brokers designated by Jones as a reward for investment research and ideas.

Because a third or more of the give-up might go to the salesman who is "supplying those good ideas," he is "likely to be very cooperative about keeping Jones informed."

Hedge funds in general "have a special ability to get a flow of good, fresh ideas about stocks from brokers—and get them early," said *Fortune*.

A Jones partner told *Dun's Review* that two of the most important reasons for the funds' success is "instant access to information from Street sources," and "the ability to make investment decisions quickly."

On the subject of information from Street sources, one

hedge fund manager told *Barron's:*[11] "Some of them are good, but we're so far down on the information dispersal list it doesn't do us that much good."

He may have been too modest about his standing on the information dispersal list, for his fund, Fairfield Partners, did appear on another list, prepared by the SEC, accusing 15 institutional customers of Merrill Lynch of violating the insider trading provisions of federal securities law. Other hedge funds on the list were A. W. Jones & Co., A. W. Jones Associates, City Associates, Hartwell Associates, Park Westlake Associates, and Fleschner Becker Associates.

It seems that while Merrill Lynch was principal underwriter for a $75 million debenture issue for Douglas Aircraft (before it merged into McDonnell Douglas), the brokerage house received information from Donald Douglas about the company's bleak earnings prospects (no profit in 1966 vs. a previously projected $3.50 to $4; about $5 in 1967 vs. $10).

The essence of the SEC charge against Merrill Lynch, reported the *Wall Street Journal,*[13] is that the nation's largest securities firm "abused its underwriting function by telling its research department the confidential information," and through its salesmen tipping off the 15 customers "before the information was publicly disclosed. The investors, in turn, have been accused by the SEC of defrauding the public in late June 1966 by selling Douglas shares or selling them short as a result of this 'inside' information."

City Associates, in order to settle its case, agreed with the SEC that it had sold short 12,100 Douglas shares between June 21 and 23, 1966, after having had "communications" with Merrill Lynch on the aircraft company's lower earnings, but City denied that these facts constituted "any wrongdoing or any violation of law."

Most of this case is still unresolved as this is written (in December 1969), but Merrill Lynch, "without admitting any wrongdoing" either, also reached a settlement with the SEC by agreeing to certain sanctions. Among the 14 officers and employees who had been accused of fraud in the case, the "most severe penalty" was meted out to Archangelo Catapano, an analyst specializing—quite appropriately, it would seem—in aerospace. The SEC *censured* him and *disassociated* him from Merrill Lynch for 60 days! Dean S. Woodman, who was at the front end of the bad news daisy chain, was merely censured.

The description of this case here does not mean to imply that the hanky-panky charged by the SEC is typical of the "investment research" attracted to the funds by all those commissions and give-ups. Somehow, though, certain phrases quoted earlier do seem to take on a deeper meaning. Consider again, if you will, "a special ability to get a flow of good, fresh ideas," and "instant access to information from Street sources," and "likely to be very cooperative," and "supplying those good ideas."

For individual investors who might be worried about trying to compete in a game where some of the players have this kind of inside information, there may be some cheer in the recent announcement that the NYSE has tightened the rules on give-ups, at least as far as outsiders are concerned. Also, the SEC, whose study of hedge funds is still going on, is reported to be interested in (among other things) the fact that private hedge funds, unlike regulated funds, have no research staffs.[34]

And don't forget, as we have already mentioned in Section 1, that those of you who are customers of brokerage houses which run private hedge funds for their members' benefit have promised you information on longs and shorts before their own hedge fund acts on it. The rest of you might look for an inside angel to help you—an *arch*angel, if you can get one.

section **FOUR**

Leverage methods

Leverage with margin
and bank borrowing

THE IMPORTANCE of leverage to hedge fund performance has already been demonstrated in detail. Briefly stated, performance is multiplied as paid-in capital is added to by leveraging. Hopefully, the thing increased is capital gain. Losses can also be increased by leverage, of course, but the main point is that the hedger who is capable enough to show a profit can *multiply* that profit simply by using leverage. The successful hedge fund manager therefore invests every dollar he can lay his hands on. Not only idle cash, but unused credit, is wasteful.

Public hedge funds are permitted to increase their capital by about 50 percent through borrowing. Some of the private hedge funds are said to use much higher leverage than 50 percent. Although the individual investor's ability to margin and borrow is limited by government regulations, his potential for increasing his leverage by options and related devices is very great indeed. The neophyte hedger should not rush into full employment of his leverage power, but he must never forget the part that leverage plays in performance, and he should set his goals accordingly. This section discusses the various methods which the hedger can use to leverage his capital and his performance.

The most common form of leverage in the stock market is buying on margin. The "margin" is the amount of cash the investor is required to advance; the balance is borrowed from the broker, who charges interest on the loan, and retains possession of the stock for collateral.

Under the Federal Reserve Board's Regulation T and current (1969) margin requirements, an investor can purchase listed stocks and listed warrants by paying 80 percent in cash and borrowing the remaining 20 percent from his broker. The buying power of $1 is therefore $1 ÷ .8, or $1.25, so the leverage possible is 25 percent.

Listed convertible bonds and listed bonds with warrants can be bought on 60 percent margin, so the leverage possible with these securities is nearly 67 percent.

Margin considerations aside, a common stock should never be bought without first checking to see if a bond convertible into the stock is available. Bonds of all kinds listed on the New York and American Stock Exchanges cover half a page in the *Wall Street Journal*. A surprising number of convertibles sell on a par with the common, and at par they are nearly always a better buy than the common, offering at least equal upside potential, less downside risk, and generally greater and safer yield. Many others sell within a small range above par, and some even drop below par for short periods. Data concerning convertible bonds can be found in the back of Standard & Poor's *Bond Guide*. Some of the advisory services, like Value Line's *Convertible Bond Service* (which will cost you extra over the basic *Investment Survey*) offer more elaborate treatment.

Bank borrowing, another form of leverage, comes under the Federal Reserve Board's Regulation U. Under the regulation, maximum bank credit for purchasing or carrying listed issues conforms to the margin requirements already mentioned, but 20 percent can also be borrowed toward the purchase of unlisted stock, and 40 percent for unlisted bonds convertible into listed stock. Only "good faith" limits—or how much are you good for?—apply to unlisted bonds convertible into unlisted stocks and unlisted bonds with warrants convertible into unlisted stocks. It may therefore be possible to use leverage even higher than 67 percent to buy these securities.

There is a cost, of course, to buying securities on credit, and that cost has been hitting successive new highs during the last few years. Margin money currently costs the investor around 10 percent, and your friendly broker compounds the charge at least monthly. Bank credit at this time is not only costly but very tight.

There are risks involved in margin buying, too. The leverage can work against you as well as for you. And there is still some risk of a margin call, possibly requiring a distress sale, but that risk now is much lower than it was at the time of the Great Crash, when margin requirements hardly deserved the name.

Under current margin rules, your broker may allow the value of the stock he holds for you to decline 73 percent before he asks for more collateral. This dreadful event need never occur if reasonable precautions are taken to limit losses.

Leverage with puts and calls

CALLS

INSTEAD of buying a stock outright or on margin, it is possible, with the expenditure of a relatively small amount of capital, to buy an *option* to buy the stock at some time in the future. The possibilities for leverage through the use of options are many times greater than those realized through buying on margin. Moreover, options offer a certain built-in protection against the risk of adverse price movements.

The most common form of stock option is the *call*, which is an option to buy 100 shares of stock at a price and within a time period mutually agreeable to buyer and seller. A call is bought in the expectation that the price of the stock will rise during the option period more than the cost of the option plus brokerage fees, so that a profit can be realized when the option is exercised or resold.

For example, a call on 100 shares of Texas Gulf Sulphur at 22, its current price, is available at a cost of $400; the option expires in 6 months and 10 days. In order for the call buyer to break even, the stock must go up $4 a share (plus brokerage fees, which we can ignore in these illustrations), and this rise must take place within the stated term of the option. If TG goes to 30, a profit of $400, or 100 percent on the money invested in the call, is realized.

If, instead of the option, the stock has been purchased outright, the entire gain of $800 goes to the investor, but his return on the $2,200 investment is only 36 percent. On the other hand, if the stock rises only $4, the outright purchase nets 18 percent on the investment, while the call results in no gain at all.

If the price of the stock remains the same or falls, the call option becomes valueless, and the buyer loses 100 percent of his investment. However, the relatively minor investment in the call is the maximum amount he can lose; the investor who buys the stock outright or on margin can lose the entire purchase price of the stock.

In order to realize a profit on a call, if the stock price goes up enough, some *action* must be taken. If TG goes from 22 to 28 in four months, say, and then drops back to 22 as the option expires, the call buyer has enjoyed no more than the temporary exhilaration of a paper profit. If he exercises the call when the stock hits 28, and sells the stock there, he nets $200 on 100 shares. Having received 100 shares at 22, he can also hold the stock for further gain, but this involves tying up much more cash, and therefore runs counter to his purpose in buying a call in the first place.

Ordinarily, it is better to sell the call itself rather than exercise the option in order to realize a profit, so that no extra cash will be required even temporarily; the put and call dealer will take it off your hands for a modest fee. There may also be tax advantages in selling the call. An option is like any other capital asset in that its tax treatment as short or long term depends upon its holding period. A profit made on a call sold after six months is a long-term gain. If a call is *exercised*, the holding period for the stock begins at the time of acquisition; the time during which the call was held goes down the drain.

The price at which a call is exercisable, called the *strike price*, can have an important bearing on its leverage potential. Ordinarily, the strike price is at or near the market price at the time the call is purchased. But many options are offered by put and call dealers, or can be negotiated, at prices "away from the market," that is, higher or lower than the current market price.

If the strike price is lower than the market price, the call costs more, because there is less risk involved for the buyer. There is also less leverage potential because of the extra cash which the call requires.

Maximum leverage is obtained by a call at a strike price higher than the market price. For example, a call on Texas Gulf Sulphur at 22 might be available for $300 if the current market price is 20, compared to a call cost of $400 if the market price is 22. Of course, the stock must rise higher, a total of 5 in this case, for the buyer to break even on the cheaper option.

During the life of the option contract, the call cost is reduced by the amount of any rights, such as dividends, payable on the stock.

PUTS

Buying a call is investing long. The short counterpart of the call is the *put,* an option to *sell,* or put, a stock at a price and within a time period agreed upon by buyer and seller. A put is purchased in the expectation that the price of the stock will fall enough during the option period so that the buyer can realize a profit.

Except for the expected direction of the price move and the fact that dividends, etc. are due *from* the holder, all of the considerations discussed for calls apply to puts also. A put is the only means by which a long-term gain can be realized on a short position, but it must be held over six months and then *sold,* not exercised.

The put is an effective device for limiting possible losses on short positions, because the maximum loss, no matter how far the ill-acting stock rises, is the amount paid for the option. "Take Puts and Sleep" might well be the slogan for those hedgers driven to insomnia by conventional shorts that bind.

USING OPTIONS

Due to the preponderance of optimists and moralists over pessimistic and uninhibited types, the demand for calls exceeds that for puts. Puts, therefore, are generally available at somewhat lower prices, with correspondingly higher leverage potentials.

The time periods for which puts and calls may be negotiated are virtually unlimited. The standard periods are 35, 65, and 95 days and 6 months and 10 days. In addition, put and call dealers have available, and often advertise, options with a wide range of strike prices and expiration dates.

The hedger need not worry too much about how options are born, and so forth; his broker, as in the case of short sales, can handle the details. One fact, however, should engage his attention at the start. The sellers, or writers, of options generally aim at, and frequently succeed in, earning at least 30 percent annually on their invested capital. Furthermore, they do this with relatively low risk. The option buyer gets the high risk along with the high profit potential. Success is dependent upon superior selection and timing. More than half of all options written expire unused, their cost prices going down the drain.

It is obvious that the profitability of puts and calls depends upon wide price moves in the stocks involved. A moderate move, even in the right direction, can still result in a loss. The stock, therefore, must be fairly volatile, but preferably not so volatile as to make timing too difficult.

The cost of an option increases along with the volatility and the option period, and also depends upon the price of the stock itself. Other factors which may affect the option price are demand, current stock price as compared to potential levels, real and imaginary, the outlook for the company, and the trend of the general market. Because of the many variables, negotiation for a favorable price can be an important part of option buying.

If the Chicago Board of Trade follows through on its proposal to establish an "Option Exchange," complete with automated trading posts, floor traders and specialists, trading in options will be facilitated and expanded. "For the first time," reports *Barron's*,[24] "firm prices will be standard operating procedure in puts and calls, and customers will be able to get out of the market as quickly as they got into it."

In the meantime, the hedger can make use of the present rather unwieldy system, applying the selection criteria mentioned. Other factors being equal, the better values tend to lie in the longer term options. *Value* in this sense could be defined as the probability that favorable market action will occur per dollar invested in an option. The long-term tax treatment on options held over six months has already been discussed.

THE OPTION HEDGE FUND

It is interesting to compare the performance of a hypothetical Option Hedge Fund with one we have already studied in Table 3, namely the 50% Hedge Fund that adjusts its "risk" or long/short ratio in response to prevailing market trends.

Table 5 shows the results of the Option Hedge Fund under exactly the same five market movements of Table 3. Also, the proportions of calls and puts in Table 5 are adjusted in the same ratio as the longs and shorts of Table 3. It is assumed that the 6/10 (6-month 10-day) options cost an average 15 percent of the value of the stocks optioned. One hundred dollars of paid-in capital therefore commands stocks worth $100 \div .15$, or $667.

In market event 1 (see Table 5), where both longs and shorts rise 30 percent, the 500 worth of optioned longs gains 150, for a net gain of 75 over the 75 cost of the calls. The 167 worth of optioned shorts drops 50, but the maximum loss possible on the puts is 25, their cost. The net gain on puts and calls for market movement 1 is therefore 50. This compares with a net gain of 24 for the adjusted "risk" 50% Hedge Fund of Table 3.

The performance results for the four remaining market movements can be followed in Table 5 without further detailed elaboration in the text. In each move, the Option Hedge Fund has a net gain over twice that of the 50% Hedge Fund of Table 3. The average return per movement is 78 percent for the Option Hedge Fund, compared to 34.5 percent for the 50% Hedge Fund, and the cumulative returns are 391 and 172.5 percent, respectively. The word *cumulative,* as before,

TABLE 5

**Hedge fund performance using puts and calls
with adjusted long/short ratios
($100 paid-in capital buys 6-month 10-day options
on stock worth $667 at 15 percent average cost)**

	Stock Value	Option Cost	Net Gain or Loss
1. L/S ratio 75–25			
Longs up 30% 500	500	75	+ 75
Shorts up 30% 167	167	25	− 25
Net change			+ 50
2. L/S ratio 27–73			
Longs down 30% 180	180	27	− 27
Shorts down 30% 487	487	73	+ 73
Net change			+ 46
3. L/S ratio 75–25			
Longs up 40% 500	500	75	+125
Shorts up 10% 167	167	25	− 25
Net change			+100
4. L/S ratio 27–73			
Longs down 10% 180	180	27	− 27
Shorts down 40% 487	487	73	+122
Net change			+ 95
5. L/S ratio 50–50			
Longs up 30% 333	333	50	+ 50
Shorts down 30% 333	333	50	+ 50
Net change			+100
Average return %			+ 78
Cumulative return %			+391

means the sum of the results of the five events using $100 paid-in capital at the start of each event.

Although the performance of the Option Hedge Fund is over twice as good as that of the 50% Hedge Fund, it is not directly proportional to the much higher leverage obtained with options. The reason for this is that *all* of the money paid for options is deducted from performance results, whether or not the options themselves pay off.

Even though a hedge fund composed entirely of puts and calls is possible, the ordinary hedger will probably choose to invest only a part of his capital in options—enough, perhaps, to increase his overall leverage to somewhere in the 50 to 200 percent area. Because wide price movements are necessary

to produce profits from options, calls should be given increased emphasis in strong bull markets, and puts in bear
markets. Both should be decreased in uncertain or sideways
movements, unless combinations (see below) are employed.
In any kind of market, of course, puts can be used to replace
shorts in order to place a positive limit on losses.

COMBINATIONS

Except for the straddle, the more esoteric combinations of
puts and calls are not used very much. A straddle is really
two options—a put and a call at the same strike price. A
spread, like the straddle, is a combination of a put and a call,
but the strike price for the put is below the current market,
while that for the call is above it.

A strip is in effect three options—two puts and one call.
The strap is one put and two calls.

All of these combination options are in themselves hedges,
and can be used with highly volatile stocks where both the
put and call features may prove profitable. Before the hedger
employs them, however, he should first gain some experience
with simple puts and calls.

Leverage with warrants

MUCH of what has been said in the preceding pages about leveraging with puts and calls applies also to stock warrants, which are traded like securities but are really just another form of option. A warrant is an option to buy unissued stock, commonly one share, upon payment of a specified sum of money (or sometimes by surrendering senior securities of the same company).

Warrants, like puts and calls, are usually bought to be sold, not exercised. Warrants are more negotiable than other options. Many warrants are listed on the American Stock Exchange and on regional exchanges; others are traded over the counter. Like common stocks, they can be traded in odd lots, and are also subject to the same margin rules.

In general, warrants have a longer life than puts and calls. The exercise price may increase at stated intervals over the life of the warrant, and stock dividends and splits can alter the exercise terms. No dividends are payable on the warrant itself.

The value of a warrant increases with the amount of time before expiration. As the expiration date approaches, the price decrease is gradual until about two years before expiration; then the market price decreases fairly steadily toward the warrant's conversion value into the common, reflecting the approaching end of the warrant's leverage potential. In other words, the premium ordinarily paid for warrants decreases quite rapidly toward zero during the last two years. The premium is the market price a warrant commands over its tangible value, or the market price minus its value upon conversion into the stock.

A warrant has no conversion value if the price of the stock is below that of the exercise price of the warrant. It is at such times, however, that the leverage potential can be greatest, provided the premium is not excessive.

In addition to the factors already mentioned, the price of a warrant is also affected by the volatility of the common stock, the outlook for the company, the degree of speculative fever, and the general trend of the market. Because of the wide range of variables, it is not possible to give an example of a typical warrant. Each one must be considered on its merits. Therefore it is not possible to demonstrate a Warrant Hedge Fund, as we did with put and call options. Suffice it to say that well-chosen warrants can add just as significantly to the leverage potential.

For the hedger, the main factor to look for in a warrant (along with projected price change) is high leverage: the highest price of common stock for the lowest cost to option it via the warrant.

For a given warrant, leverage changes with changes in the premium. Positive leverage is said to exist when a warrant has better upside than downside leverage.

The hedger will look for promising warrants to buy among those having a low price relative to the stock, high and positive leverage, favorable outlook for the common, and—necessarily—fairly substantial premiums.

Warrants selling well below conversion value and at high premiums might seem at first glance to be promising shorts. However, these very factors may favor upside leverage. Selling warrants short generally entails very high risk, and is not recommended for the hedger.

Like calls, warrants provide an absolute limit to the possible risk that is lower than that on the common, because no more than the cost of the warrant can be lost.

One possible source of information to help in the evaluation of warrants is the *Value Line Warrant Service,* issued every four weeks and covering some 70 warrants. To give one recent example, a USM Corp. warrant, expiring in 1982 and selling at $9\frac{3}{4}$, is an option to buy one share of the common at 39. The stock is selling at $37\frac{1}{2}$, so the conversion value of the warrant is zero. The premium over conversion value is therefore $9\frac{3}{4}$, or 26 percent of the price of the common. The leverage projections estimated for 25 and 50 percent rises in the common are, respectively, 61 and 136 percent increases in the price of the warrant.

Note that these increases, because of the cost of the premium, are less than the 3.8 ratio between stock and warrant prices.

USM warrants are an example of positive leverage. The downside estimates corresponding to price drops of 25 and 50 percent in the common are, respectively, 27 and 56 percent drops in the warrant.

Leverage with commodities

COMMODITY FUTURES, of course, are not stocks, but they are traded in much the same way, and they possess certain features which make them highly adaptable to hedge fund techniques.

Foremost among these features is leverage. Take copper, for example. One contract (the trading unit), consisting of 50,000 lbs., can be purchased on margin of only $1,500. Copper futures currently range between 75 and 66 cents a pound. At 70 cents a pound, one contract is worth $35,000. As the cash required is only $1,500, the effective leverage is over 2,200 percent! Try using that kind of leverage in Tables 1, 2, or 3. Performance would be 22 times better than that of the 100% Hedge Fund, for example.

The action can be very fast, also. For copper, the daily limit, or maximum daily change per contract, is 2 cents a pound. That means $1,000 a contract, or two thirds of the $1,500 invested in the margin. *In one day.*

Take another example: soybeans. A contract of 5,000 bushels, currently worth about $12,000, can be had for $500 margin. That's 2,300 percent leverage. The daily limit, or what you can win or lose on a contract, is $500, the amount of the investment in the margin.

Pork belly futures can currently be bought on 1,800 percent leverage, wheat on 1,300 percent, and even relatively stodgy commodities like silver and oats on 900 percent leverage.

In gratifying contrast to buying stocks on margin, there are no interest charges on the value of the commodity contract not covered by margin. Moreover, commissions are relatively modest, and are not due until the trade is closed out. There are no transfer taxes, and no certificates to worry about. There is no uptick rule for shorting commodities, which makes short sales easier to accomplish than is the case with stocks.

To a certain extent, selection and timing are simplified by the fact that the number of items traded and the volume of relevant information are much more limited for commodities than for stocks. Still, over 70 percent of all commodity specu-lations are said to lose money, which would indicate a high capability for misinterpretation of the available information.

The high leverage increases the risk as well as the oppor-tunity, but hedging—in the hedge fund sense of the term— seems particularly appropriate for commodity trading. (True hedging, incidentally, is more common in commodities than in stocks.)

However, some adaption must be made in setting the long/ short ratios, because commodity prices, with some exceptions, tend to move in individual seasonal patterns rather than in massive bull or bear movements. This fact can be more help than hindrance. Counter-cyclical movements will always as-sure the availability of good longs and good shorts, and the long/short ratio can be keyed to the trends of the commodities traded. The Riskop Factor described earlier can be used as a measure of risk and opportunity for commodities as well as stocks. However, if seasonal trends can be judged, it would be appropriate to substitute projected price for average price in the top line of the second term of the formula.

The subject of commodity futures deserves a book of its own; fortunately in this case, there is a recent one which can be recommended: *The Commodity Futures Trading Guide,* by Teweles, Harlow, and Stone.

A Commodity Hedge Fund, with its high leverage and fast action, certainly offers the greatest profit potential of all the hedge funds, and the greatest risk as well. The ordinary hedger might choose to put only part of his funds into com-modity futures in order to raise the overall leverage of his portfolio and limit his risk.

section **FIVE**

Do-it-yourself
and the alternatives

Private hedge funds

THIS BOOK is directed primarily to the individual who might want to use hedge fund techniques in the management of his own funds. If he does not have the time, or the desire, or the aptitude to do this, he can still enjoy (if that is the right word) participation in hedging by investing in the private or public hedge funds. This and the following discussion will examine these two alternatives, their advantages, disadvantages and costs.

A private hedge fund is an unregulated private partnership consisting of 1) general partners, who manage the fund and may or may not contribute to the pool of capital, and 2) limited partners, who are nonoperating investors in the fund. All partners who have contributed capital share proportionately in the net profits, if any, after deduction of a management fee by the general partners. They pay taxes as individuals on their proportionate shares of the dividend income and the realized capital gains.

The partnership agreements generally run for successive one-year periods, with no additions or withdrawals of capital allowed during the fiscal year. Commonly, the management fee is 20 percent of the net profit (dividends received plus capital gains less losses) taken right "off the top," as it is so neatly stated.

That 20 percent, which is several times what the ordinary mutual fund charges, might be considered quite a disadvantage by a lot of people. Nevertheless, as we have noted, many rich and sophisticated people can hardly wait to join their peers in such funds.

Let's compare the yearly fees on a net gain of 40 percent on each $100 invested. The ordinary mutual fund, charging a management fee of one half of 1 percent on the average total assets ($120) handled during the year, would come out with 60 cents per $100 invested. The hedge fund manager, taking 20 percent of the net $40 gain, would come out with $8, or over 13 times the amount that the mutual fund manager would earn on the same net gain. The investor, of course, would realize a $39.40 gain from the mutual fund, but only $32 from the hedge fund.

There must be some reason, then, why he chooses the hedge fund. ("We presume hedge fund partners are consenting adults," comments the *Financial Analysts Journal*.[27]) The reason, of course, is the *expectation*—not always realized, as we shall see later—of superior performance.

So, if you can get the Old Master, or one of *his* peers, to manage your money, it might be worth the 20 percent. Such high fees, as might be expected, do attract highly motivated fund managers, and those managers who add their own money to the investment pool should be additionally inspired.

Lest we feel too sorry for the mutual fund manager and his low percentage fee, let's remember that he may be managing $100 million or more. Let's see now, one half of 1 percent of $100 million is . . . not too bad. And he gets that fee whether or not he makes any money for the investor. Then, too, there may be a front-end load of 8 percent or so on the mutual fund —and that's not just off the top; it's off the *front*. Most of the 8 percent would go to the selling broker, however; and it's not repeated year after year, unless the investor switches mutual funds.

Although a few of the private hedge funds are said to have assets in the area of $100 million, most of them are much smaller. In nearly all cases, the number of partners is kept small—10 to 30 is considered to be about right. They want to maintain a low profile, as the saying goes, so that they can continue in unregulated bliss. But this status is threatened. According to a recent *Wall Street Journal*,[31] "the staff of the Securities and Exchange Commission advocates the close regulation of . . . hedge funds," commissioner Hugh F. Owens told a group of state securities regulators; also "the commission staff believes hedge funds should register with the commission as broker-dealers and be subject to certain reporting, record-keeping and net capital requirements from which they are currently exempt."

SEC regulation, if it comes to the hedge partnerships, will not be fatal, but it will tend to cramp their style. Regulation will most certainly hinder their operations if the restrictions go as far as those now imposed on public hedge funds.

In any case, the individual investor can go on happily using hedge fund techniques, uninhibited by any SEC regulations that may be applied to the funds.

Public hedge funds

ALTHOUGH the public hedge funds can use the same investment techniques as their private cousins—borrowing, selling short, puts and calls, high turnover, etc.—their use of these devices is limited in varying degree by self-imposed and government restrictions.

The public hedge funds which have registered to date have done so, like most other mutual funds, as regulated, open-end investment management companies under the Investment Company Act of 1940. Some have registered as diversified companies, others as nondiversified.

The Act defines a diversified company as one which meets the following requirements:

At least 75 per centum of the value of its total assets is represented by cash and cash items (including receivables), Government securities, securities of other investment companies, and other securities for the purpose of this calculation limited in respect of any one issuer to an amount not greater in value than 5 per centum of the value of the total assets of such management company and to not more than 10 per centum of the outstanding voting securities of such issuer.

The 25 percent balance of total assets is free of these limitations, so the net effect is not especially restrictive, because permissible investments in single companies are still higher than those which most fund managers would care to make anyway.

A nondiversified company, in the quaint language of the Act, means "any management company other than a diversified company."

The registration statement filed by every investment company requires a statement of policy regarding borrowing money, underwriting securities issued by others, concentrating investments in particular industries, trading in real estate and commodities, and other matters of fundamental policy.

Besides requiring registration with the SEC and regular reporting to company stockholders as well as to the SEC, the Act imposes restrictions on certain techniques important to hedge fund operations.

The most important of those affected is leverage. Bank borrowing is permitted, "Provided, that immediately after such borrowing there is an asset coverage of at least 300 per centum for all borrowing of such registered company." This seems to be the hard way to say that borrowing, or leveraging, up to 50 percent of net assets is all right.

All public hedge funds, in their registrations, have stated upper limits on the short positions they will take. These limits place a definite restriction on the efficient use of capital, as they also limit the possibility for profitability in bear markets.

A review of the prospectuses of eight representative public hedge funds reveals that the short positions of six of them are limited to a maximum of 25 percent of net assets, or gross assets less liabilities, most importantly borrowing. If the fund has borrowed its maximum 50 percent, therefore, its top permissible short position would be 25/150, or only 16.7 percent of the total funds invested, as against 83.3 percent invested long. This ratio does not permit an optimum short position in a bear market. Somewhat higher short positions, 35 percent of net assets, are permitted by the other two funds reviewed.

Three of the eight funds specify that they may use up to an additional 15 percent of net assets to go short "against the box," but this is going short against a long position in the same company's securities, so it is no help to the leveraging operation. In fact, going short against the box detracts from the efficient use of capital by a hedge fund (although it may be used to protect a gain made by a stock until it is held long enough for more favorable tax treatment).

Five of the funds specify a 10 percent limit on investments in puts and calls; one says 2 percent. Another says it will not use puts and calls at all. Warrants are limited by two funds to 5 percent and by a third to 2 percent of net assets; no limits are mentioned by the others. All promise to avoid trading in real estate and commodities, except one fund that says it may invest up to 15 percent of its assets in the latter.

Perhaps these restrictions add a note of risk-restriction to the language of the prospectuses, which uniformly confess to greater than average risk as far as operating methods are concerned. Fairly typical is the statement that the investment techniques used are "likely to involve a considerable amount of short-term trading and result in higher portfolio turnover, with increased brokerage, taxes, and other expenses, than is usual for most mutual funds. These activities also may be considered speculative and may involve greater risk of loss than the more customary investment practices in which most other mutual funds typically engage." The fund "is therefore not intended as a complete investment program and is not suitable for those investors who are unable or unwilling to assume the risks inherent in such techniques or whose objective is assured income or protection of capital."

Another typical statement is that the success of the fund "will be more dependent on the skill and ability of its management and investment adviser, and less dependent on movements in the securities markets in general, than is the case with most mutual funds."

All of the funds have as their investment objective maximum growth in share value. Some of them say they may invest in unregistered securities, commonly known as "letter stock."

The attitude toward the use of short selling is mixed, ranging from regarding it as a means to generate gains, through occasional use to offset gains or losses in the longs, to virtual abstention from its use unless everyone, including the board of directors, agrees that they're in a bear market. All the funds leave the way open to go into cash or near-cash securities when a "conservative position" seems warranted.

Everything considered, we cannot avoid the conclusion that the public hedge funds are not as well geared as their more free-swinging private counterparts to take advantage of hedge fund techniques.

Even the pursuit of favorable tax treatment imposes further restrictions on the public funds. The desired tax treatment relieves the investment company, but not its stockholders, from paying federal income tax on income which is currently distributed to its stockholders, and permits distributed long-term capital gains made by the investment company to be treated as such regardless of the holding period of the shares.

In order to qualify, the fund must derive less than 30 percent of its gross income from realized gains (without deduction for losses) on securities held less than three months, including all realized gains on short sales, and not more than 10 percent of its gross income from sources other than dividends, interest and capital gains; and it must distribute at least 90 percent of its net investment income, excluding net long-term capital gains, earned in each year.

Although the shareholders of a qualifying company receive long-term tax treatment on the distributed excess of net long-term capital gains over net short-term capital losses, any distribution from an excess of net short-term capital gain over net long-term loss is taxable to the shareholders as ordinary, or short-term, income. Dividends passed along to the shareholders are given the same treatment.

What this all seems to boil down to is that the only shareholder to benefit is the one holding fund shares for less than six months; net long-term gains can be passed on to him. In all other respects, shareholders are taxed the same as investors in private hedge funds, which is to say like any ordinary, individual investor.

The investor who wants to put his money into a hedge fund run by others, but who does not have the high price of admission required by the private funds, has little choice but to invest in the public hedge funds. He might console himself with the thought that at least he's not paying the 20 percent off the top of net gain usually taken by private fund management. Let's look at that.

The *Los Angeles Times,*[15] in an article titled "Here's a Peek at What Happens in Hedge Funds," asked what it called "one obvious question." Why should the managers of a public hedge fund "take a smaller management fee—it will range from a minus fee to 4% of assets depending on [performance] —than the 20% in private management?"

The fund president interviewed "says it took a bit of selling," according to the financial newsman, who should have taken another peek. Although the president may rate high marks for salesmanship, the *Times* man apparently missed the point that the 20 percent enjoyed by private hedge fund managers is 20 percent of net *profits,* while the 4 percent limit on the public hedge fund is 4 percent of the net *assets* managed. He might have asked another obvious question: Why 4 percent of net assets instead of the one half of 1 percent charged by most mutual funds?

The hedge fund under discussion starts out with a *base* management fee of one half of 1 percent of the average net asset value of the fund during any year. This is subject to an *incentive adjustment* which may be positive or negative, depending upon performance.

According to the prospectus, "the positive incentive adjustment, if any, will equal 20% of the number of percentage points by which . . . the Fund exceeds that of the [S & P's 500] Index . . . multiplied by the average net asset value of the Fund in such year," but not to exceed $3\frac{1}{2}$ percent of average net assets (except where there has been a negative adjustment carryover).

In other words, under favorable circumstances, fund management can do quite well—just how well will be shown in a moment. The fund, unlike the private hedge fund, bases its fee on the *average* (and hopefully increasing) net assets managed *throughout* the year. Also, while the private fund bases its fee on a *positive increase* in assets, this one rates its performance against the Standard & Poor's 500, which may decline.

A few examples will illustrate. First, let's assume no net change in the Index during the year, but an increase in share value, including any capital gains distributions, of 17.5 percent, which will result in an "excess performance differential" of 17.5 percent, and an "incentive adjustment" of exactly $3\frac{1}{2}$ percent. Added to the one half of 1 percent base management fee, the maximum 4 percent is achieved.

Each $100 invested in the fund at the start of the year increases to $117.50 at the close. If the increase has been fairly uniform, the average net assets managed during the year is $108.75, and 4 percent of that—the total management fee—is $4.35. As a percentage of the $17.50 gain, the $4.35 fee is nearly 25 percent, compared to the 20 percent a private hedge fund might take.

For gains greater than 17.5 percent, the 4 percent limit applies and the management fee, expressed as a percentage of net gain, decreases steadily—to 6 percent, for example, if the shares double in value. The fee is therefore $6 on a $100 gain, compared to $4.35 on a $17.50 gain. We might say that the management incentive, expressed as a percentage of shareholder gain, decreases with that gain.

Indeed, on gains of less than 17.5 percent, the proportionate share of management is even greater. On a 10 percent gain, the fee would be 2.5 percent of the average $105 managed, or 26 percent of the gain itself. Management would take over 33 percent of a 4 percent gain, and over 45 percent of a 2 percent gain.

All of the above examples assume no change in the Index. If the Index rises 10 percent, net asset gain must be 27.5 percent to reach the 4 percent management fee maximum limit. At that point, the fee is over 16 percent of the gain. As before, the fee, as a percentage of the gain, decreases as the gain increases, and increases as the gain decreases.

If the Index *decreases* 27.5 percent and the fund's net assets decrease 10 percent, the fund has still out-performed the Index by +17.5 percent. Even though the shareholder has lost

10 percent, the management fee is still 4 percent of the average $95 managed, and the fee is $3.80.

However, because the fund lost money, the incentive fee is not payable immediately, but is carried forward as much as three years, until asset appreciation makes it possible to liquidate the charge. Not more than 4 percent may be paid in any one year, but "Any portion of the base fee and incentive adjustment which is not paid in the year when earned because of payment of carried forward fees will also be carried forward for not more than three years and then paid on [a] first earned, first paid basis."

If the fund performs worse than the Index, a negative incentive adjustment is calculated in the same manner as the positive one, and is applied to reduce the base fee. The 4 percent limit on this adjustment applies also. If the "negative incentive adjustment exceeds the base fee, the base fee will be reduced to zero and the unapplied balance . . . will be carried forward one year in reduction of the positive incentive adjustment, if any (but not the base fee)."

If there is a loser the next year also, in other words, the previous year's negative adjustment is forgiven. The shorter carry forward for negative adjustments compared to positive ones doesn't strike us as very sporting.

All but one of the public hedge funds examined have some form of incentive compensation for management. Five of the eight, including the one reviewed above, place an upper limit on their management fees of 4 percent of the average net assets. The others have limits of 1⅛ percent, 1 percent, and three fourths of 1 percent.

Five of the funds base their performance on the Standard & Poor's 500-stock Index, one on the NYSE Composite Index, one on net realized gains, and the last bases its fee solely on average net assets.

Front-end loads, or sales commissions, for six of the funds range from 7.5 to 8.75 percent; two have none. One fund charges a redemption fee.

The funds reviewed have not been identified by name, because it is not the purpose here to provide a comprehensive rating system, but rather to cite enough examples to demonstrate: 1) the significant characteristics they have in common, 2) the range of differences within the group, particularly as to cost, but also with respect to such matters as investment approaches and restrictions, and 3) how they compare with other investment alternatives.

With this background, the decision on whether or not to invest in a public hedge fund should be facilitated. If the decision is to do so, we hope that some stimulus has been provided toward a close examination of the fund's prospectus (or registration statement) as well as its operating performance to date.

The bear market nightmare— or what went wrong?

WHEN *Barron's*[11] interviewed the manager of Fairfield Partners, a private hedge fund which had more than doubled its assets in three years, he had this to say about hedging: "By hedging our positions, what we're doing is using speculative techniques to conservative ends. What this really means is that we're not gambling on the market."

Really? If "not gambling" means not taking risks, he cast some doubt on this a few questions and answers later, when he said, "One big fallacy to hedge funds is that people think you can't lose with them. Obviously you can. You can lose with a vengeance, and you can lose not only in a bad market but in a good market, too."

Asked about what would happen in a two-year bear market, he said, "We'd lose money just like everybody else." This statement was made about one-half year before the start of the 1969 bear market.

Other warnings had been sounded, beginning with the earliest articles on hedge funds. The *Business Week* piece that appeared in 1966 commented, "Hedge funds so far have done well, although they have never been tested in a prolonged bear market."

Later that same year *Dun's Review* wrote,

One striking thing about many of the more aggressive fund operators is that they have no firsthand knowledge of the memorable sell-off of 1962. Many of today's funds, in short, are dominated by 25-year-olds fresh out of Harvard Business School or the equivalent—bright, hard-working youngsters who are too new at the game to remember 1962, to say nothing of earlier market setbacks. One hedger, at 42, confesses: They make me feel like an old man.

Of course, when Galbraith said that financial genius consists of a short memory and a rising market, he had in mind a larger group of inspired money managers than the youngsters fresh out of his own school.

The article in *Dun's Review* quoted one hedge fund manager to the effect that "unfortunately, the business is going to draw some people who aren't [good portfolio managers], and some individuals may get hurt."

Enough of dire prophecy. How fared the hedge funds— public and private, and run by a mixed bag of managers—in the bear market of 1969?

Early in August, the *Wall Street Journal*[21] put the matter neatly in the story's headline: "Hedge Fund Heebie-Jeebies: Stock Market a Short-Seller's Dream? More Like a Nightmare, Say Professionals."

It is doubtful that the term *heebie-jeebies* has been mentioned in a newspaper since the era of the Great Crash. The affliction was rampant at that time, but we had come to believe that it had been completely stamped out. Certainly no wonder drugs have been exploited for its treatment; the heebie-jeebies era was long before the term *wonder drugs* was coined. The headlining of the new outbreak suggested the gravity of the situation.

The article confirmed this: "Among some of the private hedge funds, asset losses this year have run to as much as 40% through July, and setbacks of 25% and 35% are said to be fairly common. In contrast, the Dow-Jones industrial average fell about 14% in the same period, and the average non-hedged mutual fund 18%. In one large private partnership, the decline in June alone was 17%."

We suspect that anyone old enough to remember the original heebie-jeebies got at least a little satisfaction in reporting that "Partners who entered with visions of 'hot' young money managers parlaying their investments into big capital gains have been withdrawing in disappointment. Wall Street sources say some of the less-seasoned private partnerships are simply going out of existence."

Some of the afflicted investors might even be justified in terming their particular operations "mutual funds for the *formerly* rich." Actually, perhaps unknowingly, they were acquiring "sophistication," that investor attribute so coveted by hedge fund managers. One told the *Journal*, "The sophisticated investor we're aiming at doesn't measure anything by a short-term swing, and it's only those who have joined partnerships in more recent times who are withdrawing."

As it is used by fund managers, the word *sophisticated* takes on a commendatory or complimentary coloration, and apparently implies a willingness to absorb financial punishment, if not actually to enjoy a beneficial sensation while doing so. Those disgruntled investors who have checked their dictionaries to confirm that the word means "worldly-wise, disillusioned," may perhaps be forgiven for protesting, "You've sophisticated me enough already!"

Among the public hedge funds mentioned by the *Journal*, and ranked by Arthur Lipper Corp., the Hubshman Fund was off 39 percent during the first seven months of 1969, Blair Fund was off nearly 22 percent, and Hedge Fund of America was off 26 percent.

The *best* performance was by the newest entrant, Berger-Kent Special Fund, which had begun operating on April 22. It declined 14.5 percent, compared to an 11.2 percent drop in the Dow-Jones industrial average during the same period. In addition to its shorter time exposure to the bear market, Berger-Kent owed some of its "best" rating to keeping 35 to 40 percent of its assets in cash equivalents since its inception. The 14.5 percent decline in total assets is therefore much less than the price drop in its stocks. The maximization of this technique is obviously to go 100 percent cash, and avoid stocks completely.

Such a resort to cash, as we have seen, violates one of the fundamental reasons for the hedge funds' superior profit potential, the use of leverage to stay fully invested at all times. Cash is sinful to the orthodox hedger.

However, the *Journal* reported that the other funds, inspired perhaps by the record of Berger-Kent, were also maintaining heavy cash positions. Even some of the pros running the private hedge funds "are giving cash an increasingly defensive role, letting it run to 50% or more of assets." Mount Vernon Associates "has about 45% of assets in cash and may let its cash position build to 60% or 70%."

The reader can try those figures on his Table 1—under Mutual Fund, of course, not Hedge Fund. A manager who takes shelter in a high cash position is not running a hedge fund; he's merely running. To put it within our context of hedge fund criteria, not only is he failing to use leverage, he is even failing to use his paid-in capital efficiently, and is tacitly (but nonetheless loudly) admitting his shortcomings in selection and timing.

It is also instructive to try to determine, from the various managers' remarks quoted in the *Journal*, why the "short-seller's dream" was for them more like a nightmare.

Those managers who are "rampaging bulls who aren't comfortable shorting" might do better, we can surmise, by shifting to mutual funds where no shorting is allowed, especially if their discomfort extends to the visceral regions.

"We feel better in this kind of market being in liquid assets rather than being short," says one manager. "If there's a rebound, the market can turn up rapidly, and being heavily short could be damaging." In addition to his high cash position he has been keeping his short position down to 2 or 3 percent. "We plan to leave it that way for now," he says.

Giving in to his fear that a rapid upturn might rip his shorts has effectively eliminated the profit potentials of both selling short and shifting the long/short ratio in order to keep in tune with the market. He is also admitting his inability to select suitable shorts during a period when they were abundantly available.

Some of the fund managers who tried selling short on a larger scale seem to have an ill-defined sense of having been let down by something in which they had placed their confidence.

"Shorting doesn't seem to give you the help you need in this kind of market," says one.

Another commented that even though his fund "ran a ratio of 70% short and 30% long" in recent months in the sharply falling market, "the short positions weren't producing the results expected from them."

So turning away from the short hedge, the managers of this fund "have moved toward larger cash positions . . . until they are satisfied that a definite market trend is taking hold." One partner explained to the *Journal*, "With this market you only tend to whipsaw yourself."

In the above case, the clear as well as the probable shortcomings in the areas of leverage, short selling, adjusting the long/short ratio, and selection and timing are obvious to the reader.

Why the short positions weren't producing "the results expected of them" is probably explained in large part by the complaint about whipsawing, which is a word used by professionals who want to avoid the more degrading "poor selection and timing." Even as a euphemism it doesn't sound too good.

Poor selection lies in picking a stock with the qualities detailed earlier, when we considered "The High-Fliers As Shorts." Given these qualities of high volatility, high and nervous short interest, and so forth, whipsawing—repeatedly buying and selling the wrong stock at the wrong time—comes easily.

This assessment is reinforced by complaints about "the shrinking marketability of stocks that some of [the fund managers] have encountered during the recent market decline."

"Bids for stocks disappeared on the downside," one manager is quoted by the *Journal*, "and getting bids on some stocks was practically impossible." It's hard to believe, with *somebody* buying about 11 million shares of Big Board stocks alone every day, and with daily upticks indicated for nearly every stock, that these difficulties existed for more than a handful of stocks. We get more than a hint of the Lemming Syndrome rampant.

A sympathetic broker is quoted: "When you have a lot of people with a lot of money operating in the same stocks, you can't really go short in large amounts."

One of the fund managers who "has found little or no use for leveraging this year" complains, quite rightly, about the 9 or 10 percent interest on borrowing. "If interest rates stay high, we may use put and call options more heavily," he says.

Puts and calls may limit his losses, as we have seen in Section Four, but we also noted the greater skill needed in selection and timing if options are to be profitable. Because the large drop in his fund's assets already indicates problems in selection and timing, it is not easy to see how greater concentration on puts and calls would improve performance.

We have now analyzed, within the framework of this book's criteria for hedge fund performance, just about every excuse advanced by the managers quoted in the *Journal's* Heebie-Jeebies article. This analysis was not made in order to disparage any particular fund manager; their names were omitted. The analysis was made in order to demonstrate to the reader what can happen to performance when hedge fund principles are not adhered to, and also to give the neophyte hedger confidence that the competition is not as tough as he might have assumed.

The *Journal* noted that the postmortem on hedge fund performance provided no consensus among fund managers and analysts beyond the fact that "It's a tough market." The unsophisticated, or recently sophisticated, investor might be forgiven for replying, "Okay, it's a tough market—but you professional hedge fund managers are supposed to know how to operate in tough markets, and especially in bear markets. In *easy* markets, *I* can make money, and without paying you 20 percent."

We should not leave the *Journal* article without pointing out that at least one of the fund managers quoted retains his faith in hedge fund principles. "I think the concept has been vindicated," he says. "We're down less than many mutual funds, and we've been able to make money—several million dollars—in short sales. The concept is good; it's our management of it that we hope to improve."

Also, the Fairfield Partners man, whose interview by *Barron's* was noted at the opening of this discussion, had the following to say about cash and leverage:

Q. What is the hedge fund's attitude toward cash?
A. Very simple. We shouldn't have any.
Q. Does it work out that way?
A. Usually. From time to time . . . we do find ourselves sitting on some cash, but we try to be fully invested.
Q. Does fully mean 140%?
A. Yes. Any time we have buying power, we either should be selling something short or buying something.

We trust that a follow-up interview by *Barron's* will tell us about the application of these principles during the 1969 bear market, and the results in terms of performance.

Advantages in running
your own hedge fund

THE PROSPECTUSES of the public hedge funds always contain some statement along the following lines: By buying shares in the fund, an investor may receive advantages he would not really obtain as an individual, including professional management and continuous supervision of investments.

May is the key word here. "Remember the *May*." The prospectuses also warn: Advance assurance cannot be given that the fund's investment objectives will be realized or that the value of the fund's shares will increase.

In the light of the preceding pages, that seems like an understatement.

Private hedge funds also offer professional management and continuous supervision, and cannot guarantee gains—and that, too, has been demonstrated.

Both types seem excessively expensive: the private funds with their 20 percent off the top, and the public funds with, as a rule, about 8 percent off the front, and some of those with incentive fees able under certain conditions to charge even more than 20 percent of the net gain. The high charges alone should be enough to encourage the individual investor to manage his own capital—or at least that part of it which he can afford to risk in this manner—as a private, individual hedge fund.

Besides saving the high fees, there are other advantages for the individual investor-hedger.

Consider leverage. The individual hedger is not subject to any of the limitations imposed on the public hedge funds. He can leverage as much as the private hedge fund. Using the methods detailed in this book, he can leverage just as high as he wishes, consonant with the risk he is willing to assume.

Consider selection and timing. Although the hedger may not be able to match the top managers of private hedge funds, he should—by sticking to hedge fundamentals—be able to do better than a lot of them, and their public counterparts, as well. By using the newly devised Riskop Factor described in this book, the reader can improve his edge on most fund managers in the matter of measuring risk and opportunity in stock selection and timing.

Consider short selling. Since no one, by common admission, does this well, it offers a great field of opportunity for the individual hedger. Moreover, if he's not managing multi-millions, he needn't worry about getting off his relatively modest short sales. For the same reason, he can easily short stocks which do not trade in the high volume sought by the pro managers.

Consider adjustment of the long/short ratio. By using the method described in Section Three (and so far as we know not used by anyone else to date) the individual hedger can keep his portfolio attuned to the market trend, and also avoid missing market turns.

Consider maneuverability and *taxes.* The small hedger has the obvious edge in these matters also. He can take profits on short-term gains where the upside potential has been realized, and on short sales, using turnover to compound his return on assets.

With these advantages, the use of hedge fund techniques should result in a marked improvement in the performance of even the presently successful private investor, and also, we hope, provide the means for the present also-ran to move into the winner's circle.

In short, if the investor is going to be in the stock market at all, he'd better have a good understanding of hedge fund techniques, because they do provide the tools for superior profit potential.

To conclude with a few words on getting started: The neophyte hedger, even if he is an experienced trader, would be well advised to begin with a paper portfolio, continuing his dry runs until he has confidence in his new tools. A little experimentation will develop the method for adjusting the long/short ratio most suitable for his requirements.

If the dry runs do not provide enough incentive, actual trading in a few shares (say 1 to 10) of each of the portfolio stocks should provide the necessary stimulus. The transition to larger and more profitable long and short positions can then be made with confidence.

Epilogue

AT SEVERAL points throughout this book reference was made to the *Fortune* article, "The Jones Nobody Keeps Up With,"[1] an article that has been given major credit for the subsequent proliferation of the hedge funds. As the writing of this book neared completion, *Fortune* published its second article on the funds (by the same author), "Hard Times Come to the Hedge Funds,"[35] which gives further documentation to the dismal performance record of the hedge funds during the 1969 bear market. Although the second article, which presents some of the adverse factors already discussed in this book, may well serve to dampen the growth rates of both the private and public hedge funds, it also serves to reinforce the main theme of this book, namely, that the most promising field for growth in the use of hedge fund techniques lies with the individual investors for whom this book was written.

This is not to say that the growth of the private and public hedge funds should be permanently inhibited. In spite of the restrictions—present and threatened—on them, the hedge funds still possess superior profit *potential*, provided the fundamentals are observed. But what the fund managers must deal with now—and perhaps they didn't plan it quite that way—are some truly sophisticated (read *disillusioned*) investors who will no longer accept without question the excessive management fees levied in the past. As a selling point, the magic has evaporated from the hedge fund story—forever, we hope. Even some of the professional hedge fund managers seem to have increased their own degree of sophistication, having discovered that 20 percent of nothing is nothing.

It seems reasonable to assume that the future growth of the organized hedge funds will be closely related to more reasonable fees plus convincing evidence of sustained, superior performance—based, of course, on adherence to basic hedge fund principles.

We were saddened to read, in the second *Fortune* piece, that 1969 dealt rather unkindly even with the Old Master, Alfred Winslow Jones, the man who started it all. Although his two funds made healthy gains in the fiscal years ending May 31, 1966, 1967 and 1968, by May 31, 1969 Jones could only report a "break-even performance" to his investors, compared to a 4.3 percent rise in the New York Stock Exchange composite average. By October 1, 1969 the Jones funds (along with City Associates, run by former Jonesmen) were down between 30 and 40 percent, compared with a 13 percent drop in the NYSE composite.

Jones confesses that he was caught up in what he called the "euphoria" of the times leading up to the bear market break—even questioning the hedging value of his shorts, and evidently cutting way back on them. (Naturally, he had not heard of the Thomas Euphoria Index.)

"It was in this frame of mind," notes *Fortune*, "that Jones came into late 1968 and into the market top, which, of course, could not at the time be easily recognized as such." (The method of setting the ratio of longs to shorts suggested in this book indicates a 50/50 ratio going into November 1968, a peak of 58/42 during the last week of that month, a return to 50/50 during the last third of December, and a long/short ratio of 41/59 by early January 1969. The NYSE composite average peaked at 61.27 on November 29, 1968 and tumbled to a January low of 56.77 on the 13th day of 1969.)

As the market slide continued, "Jones and his portfolio managers gradually cut back their risk by building up short positions," but it was "too little, too late." By May 31, 1969, "all of the early gains of the fiscal year had been wiped out." Still later, as we have noted, things got really bad.

Jones, of course, had plenty of company in his suffering. *Fortune* also noted figures compiled by John M. Hartwell, investment counselor and hedge fund manager, regarding eight hedge funds (including the two he runs) which he kept track of. During June 1969 the eight funds dropped an average 15.3 percent (compared to 6.9 percent for the NYSE composite); they dropped another 10 percent in July (against 6.4 percent for the NYSE). During a brief market lift in August, the funds reporting failed to match the gain of the NYSE composite. (Some hedge fund managers have been trying to boost morale by maintaining that their funds, having fallen faster, will come back faster than the general market.)

Disaster also struck among the public hedge funds. For example, Hedge Fund of America, with a 24 percent decline through November of 1969, placed 340th in a tabulation of 379 mutual funds by Arthur Lipper Corp. The hapless Hubshman Fund, the pioneer of the public hedge funds, lost 47 percent for the 11-month period, "taking firm possession of the 379th spot," as *Fortune* phrased it. (The departures of these and other hedge fund managers from what this book considers basic hedge fund principles have already been noted in the last section.)

Some of the private hedge funds with poor records during the 1969 bear market have simply gone out of business, their investors apparently having suffered more sophistication than they could bear. "No one knows how many hedge funds have folded," says *Fortune*. "But a fair number have." It mentions New York's Haymar Associates and Los Angeles' Associates West, both of which got their investment advice from a subsidiary of Hayden, Stone Inc., the prominent brokerage house. Also leaving the scene, "albeit slowly," is New York's Woodpark Associates, which has been having trouble unloading the unregistered stock in its portfolio.

The blame for the dismaying performance records of most of the hedge funds during the 1969 bear market is placed overwhelmingly on short selling (where they should have been cleaning up like grunion hunters at spawning time). Some managers have lost faith in the whole idea. "Hedging is vastly overrated as a concept," *Fortune* quotes Mr. Hartwell. "People argue that there is psychological comfort in having a short position . . . I stopped believing it after we got bloody and beaten from short selling."

Others, including Jones and the managers of City Associates and Fairfield Partners, are staunch in their defense of the hedge concept, blaming their setbacks not on the concept itself, but on their own inability to apply it properly. (Oddly enough, however, they still seem to regard hedging more as a necessity for keeping the "nerve" to operate aggressively on the long side, rather than as a source of profits from the shorts.) As *Fortune* noted, "the great majority of stocks went down last year, and . . . there were innumerable opportunities to clean up on the short side—if only the opportunities had been seized." Although the few good shorts that were discovered tended to become overcrowded (the Lemming Syndrome rampant), the hedge funds' main problem, as *Fortune* put it so clearly, was elementary: "they simply picked the wrong stocks to short" (in our context, poor selection and timing).

We trust that this recital of the hedge funds' woes will serve to deepen further the reader's respect for basic hedge fund principles.

Sources

(Listed in order of publication)

1. "The Jones Nobody Keeps Up With," Carol J. Loomis, *Fortune*, Apr. 1966.

2. "Funds That Use Short Sale Tactics," *Business Week*, Apr. 2, 1966.

3. "Hedge Fund Management: A New Respectability for Short Selling," Martin T. Sosnoff, *Financial Analysts Journal*, July–Aug. 1966.

4. "Heyday of the Hedge Funds," *Dun's Review*, Jan. 1968.

5. "Market Place: Market Hedging and the Funds," *New York Times*, Feb. 20, 1968.

6. "Big Board Warns Hedge Fund Trading Rise Imperils Finances of Some Member Firms," Richard Rustin, *Wall Street Journal*, Apr. 3, 1968.

7. "The Hedge Funds: More Competition?" *Magazine of Wall Street*, Apr. 27, 1968.

8. "Hedge Funds: Investing Partnerships Grow, Draw Scrutiny by Exchanges and SEC," Richard Rustin, *Wall Street Journal*, May 20, 1968.

9. "American Exchange Starts Member Poll on Hedge-Fund Role," *Wall Street Journal*, May 21, 1968.

10. "Hedge Funds: Prickly," *Economist*, May 25, 1968.

11. "Fully Invested: That's the Long and Short of It for Barton Biggs and His Hedge Fund," *Barron's*, July 8, 1968.

12. "Unhedged Judgments: Barton Biggs Discusses Some of His Longs and Shorts," *Barron's*, July 15, 1968.

13. "SEC Hearing Is Told Merrill Lynch Official Said Data Were Passed," *Wall Street Journal*, Dec. 17, 1968.

14. "Up and Down Wall Street," Alan Abelson, *Barron's*, Feb. 24, 1969.

15. "Inside the Market: Here's a Peek at What Happens in Hedge Funds," Ernest A. Schonberger, *Los Angeles Times*, Mar. 4, 1969.

16. "Securities Regulators Express Concern about Hedge Funds," *Wall Street Journal*, Mar. 10, 1969.

17. "Hubshman Management Corp., Top Officer Penalized by SEC for Federal Violations," *Wall Street Journal*, Mar. 24, 1969.

18. "Inside the Market: Knack of Hedging," Ernest A. Schonberger, *Los Angeles Times*, Mar. 30, 1969.

19. "The Sargeant Wears Two Hats," *Forbes*, Apr. 15, 1969.

20. "American Board Finds Its Rules Adequate to Cover Members' Hedge Fund Activities," *Wall Street Journal*, Apr. 28, 1969.

21. "Hedge Fund Heebie-Jeebies: Stock Market Drop a Short-Seller's Dream? More Like a Nightmare Say Professionals," *Wall Street Journal*, Aug. 8, 1969.

22. "Mutual Funds: Annual Performance Ratings," *Forbes*, Aug. 15, 1969.

23. "Performance Funds: Under a Cloud," *Forbes*, Aug. 15, 1969.

24. "Option Pick-Up: Fresh Capital, New Ideas Spur the Put-and-Call Trade," Margaret D. Pacey, *Barron's*, Sept. 22, 1969.

25. "Clipped Hedge: Long or Short, Says Leo Goldner, The Stock Market Is Risky," *Barron's*, Sept. 22, 1969.

26. "Look, Don't Touch: It's Time to Draw Up Shopping Lists, Says Leo Goldner, Not to Buy," *Barron's*, Sept. 29, 1969.

27. "Trading Partnerships—Hedges or Hogs?" Irving Kahn, *Financial Analysts Journal*, Sept.–Oct. 1969.

28. "The Funds," *Forbes*, Oct. 1, 1969.

29. "Three Customers of Merrill Lynch Face License Loss: SEC Staff Urges the Action Against Investment Firms in Douglas Aircraft Case, Penalty for 12 Others Urged," *Wall Street Journal*, Oct. 10, 1969.

30. "Up And Down Wall Street," Alan Abelson, *Barron's,* Oct. 13, 1969.

31. "Close Regulation of Hedge Funds Is Backed by SEC Staff; Study Is Now Under Way," *Wall Street Journal,* Oct. 22, 1969.

32. "Modern Moneyman: A Hedge Fund Manager Mixes Research, Risks to 'Perform' in Market," *Wall Street Journal,* Oct. 31, 1969.

33. "1929 And 1969: Financial Genius Is a Short Memory and a Rising Market," John Kenneth Galbraith, *Harper's,* Nov. 1969.

34. "Offshore and On: The SEC's Reach Threatens to Exceed Its Grasp," Henry G. Manne, *Barron's,* Nov. 3, 1969.

35. "Hard Times Come to the Hedge Funds," Carol J. Loomis, *Fortune,* Jan. 1970.

index

Index

Hedge Funds, Mutual Funds and Super Funds, 24
Hedging, 3, 4, 10, 30, 40, 64, 89, 152; *see also* Adjusting the long/short ratio *and* "Risk"
  advantages, 76, 78
  vs. leverage, importance of, 39–40
  not really being used, 75–76
  as term is used by hedge funders, 4–5
Heritage Fund, 10
How I Made Millions in Three-Quarter Time, 58
Hubshman Fund, 10, 24, 68, 139, 151

I

Indexes, 53, 89–93, 135
Indicator Digest and *Technical Stock Reports*, 48, 89
Information gap, 23–25
Investment Analysis and Portfolio Management, 58
Investment companies, open-end, 3, 10, 129–36; *see also* Mutual funds
Investment Company Act of 1940, 129–30
Investors Overseas Services, 21

J

Jones, Alfred Winslow, 7, 9, 10, 19, 23, 76, 79, 97, 99, 149, 150, 151; *see also* Old Master
Jones, A. W., & Co., 100
Jones, A. W., & Associates, 100

K

Kellwood Co., 19
Kennedy, Joseph P., 60
Kerr-McGee, 79, 82, 83, 86

L

Lemming Syndrome, 52–53, 142, 152
Leverage, 4, 30, 43–44, 105–22, 130, 140, 142, 146
  methods, 105–22
    with commodities, 121–22
    with margin and bank borrowing, 105–7
    with puts and calls, 109–15
    with warrants, 117–19
Leverage fund, 39–40, 45–46

Lipper, Arthur, Corp., 139, 151
Lockheed, 71
Loew's Theatres, 19
Long/short ratio; *see* Adjusting the long/short ratio
Los Angeles Times, 23, 96, 133
Losses, cutting, 55

M

McDonnell Douglas, 71, 100
McKinsey & Co., 20
Mackay, Charles, 55
Maneuverability and turnover, 30, 95–97, 146
Margin, 66, 105–7
Merrill Lynch, 100–101
Milgo Electronics, 85, 86
Money Game, The, 55
Moody's, 57
Mount Vernon Associates, 53, 140
Moving averages, 90–93
Mutual funds, ix, 3, 5, 10, 31, 33–34, 43, 126, 129–36

N

Natomas, 79
New York Stock Exchange, x, 11, 13, 15, 49, 89, 101
New York Times, 10, 61, 89

O

Occidental Petroleum, 16
Old Master, 8, 31, 54, 61, 75, 88, 126, 150; *see also* Jones, Alfred Winslow
100% Hedge Fund, 34–38, 43
Oppenheimer & Co., 14
Opportunity, 80, 81; *see also* Riskop Factor
Option Exchange, 112
Option Hedge Fund, 113–15
Options; *see also* Puts; Calls; *and* Warrants
  combinations, 115
  using, 111–13
Owens, Hugh F., 127

P

Pacific Coast Stock Exchange, 64
Pan American Sulphur Co., 71–72, 85, 86

This book may be kept

39828